APPROACHES
TO ANTHROPOSOPHY

RUDOLF STEINER

RUDOLF STEINER

APPROACHES
TO ANTHROPOSOPHY

*Human Life from the
Perspective of Spiritual Science*

Two lectures given in Liestal, Basle,
11th January and 16th October 1916

Translated by Simon Blaxland-de Lange

RUDOLF STEINER PRESS

Translated by Simon Blaxland-de Lange from
Die Aufgabe der Geisteswissenschaft und deren Bau in Dornach
and
Das menschliche Leben vom Gesichtspunkte der Geisteswissenschaft

Two Lectures taken from
Philosophie und Anthroposophie Gesammelte Aufsätze 1904 – 1923
Bibliography Number 35 in the Complete German Edition
of the works of Rudolf Steiner

Edited by Joan M. Thompson

ISBN 1 85584 151 7

Typeset by Imprint, Crawley Down
Printed and Bound in Great Britain by
WBC Limited, Bridgend, Mid Glamorgan

CONTENTS

APPROACHES TO ANTHROPOSOPHY

THE MISSION OF SPIRITUAL SCIENCE AND OF ITS BUILDING AT DORNACH

HUMAN LIFE FROM THE PERSPECTIVE OF SPIRITUAL SCIENCE

NOTES

THE MISSION OF SPIRITUAL SCIENCE AND OF ITS BUILDING AT DORNACH, SWITZERLAND

PREFACE

The substance of what follows is the report of a lecture which I gave in response to a lecture from another quarter, where a series of objections were pronounced against the views summed up under the name 'Anthroposophy' or 'spiritual science'.

I came to know of these objections through the circumstance that the lecturer himself had them printed in a newspaper. When the context of the observations that follow is borne in mind, it might seem as if their special publication were unjustified. With regard to this it may be said that, even though the objections in question were, to begin with, only the subject of a single lecture, they are the ones with which it is repeatedly intended from many quarters to refute the spiritual science (Anthroposophy) that is the theme of the present essay. They are to a certain extent typical 'refutations'. They are typical, not only because of what is alleged, but because of the *manner* in which an attitude is taken towards that to which objections are raised. This manner is characteristic. It is often the case that people do not fix their attention upon what spiritual science says and direct their attack against this, but fabricate an idea of what they *think* it says, and then attack this idea. A curious situation results.

The one attacked may quite agree with his opponent in his judgement of all that is attacked, and yet he is obliged to find that he is condemned together with the distorted idea formed of him. The following example is particularly characteristic of this form of attack. A building is being erected for the purposes of Anthroposophy. This is to serve as a 'School of Spiritual Science'. In the artistic form of the building it is sought to realize that for which this spiritual science can give the stimulus. The building is intended to bring to artistic expression that for which it provides the frame. Certainly, the manner in which this is accomplished may be objected to from one or another artistic point of view. Indeed, the present author is far from thinking that what is being striven for by means of this building could be achieved to everyone's satisfaction. But he is endeavouring to see that every sort of inartistic symbolism or allegorizing is kept far removed from it. It is only necessary to open one's eyes in order to observe that there is absolutely nothing symbolical or allegorical of the kind often met with where, not spiritual science — such as is to be pursued in this building — but unhealthy mysticism or such-like makes itself felt. Yet, in spite of this, one of the objections raised against this building is: Anyone who enters this building will find all kinds of mysterious symbols which are incomprehensible to the non-initiated, etc., etc. In this way what we wish to attain in the building is successfully attacked, but only through the attack being directed against something which does not exist, and which, if it were really so, the one attacked would repudiate just as his opponent does. But by far the larger part of what is adduced against spiritual science is on these lines. First a caricature of it is made, which flies in the face of all scientific thinking, and then this caricature is attacked with the weapons of science. Another caricature is made, which is attacked from the point of view of religious feeling; whereas in truth no religious confession would have the slightest occasion to think anything but kindly of spiritual science, if its true form were kept in view instead of a caricature of it.

In such a state of affairs it is almost impossible to do anything more than meet these attacks by stating the actual aims and characteristics of anthroposophical spiritual science. I endeavoured to do this in the lecture upon which this essay is based. Above all it is shown that the attacks are inapposite, because they are directed against self-made targets and not against that of which they speak.

Thus, in this essay, the true form of spiritual science is delineated in contradistinction to the imaginary one.

In the *Afterword*, a further point is added which amplifies the hints given in the lecture. The word 'we' often occurs in the lecture; this is because I spoke to a certain extent as the representative of the movement in which Anthroposophy is cultivated.

Rudolf Steiner
April 1916

THE MISSION OF SPIRITUAL SCIENCE AND OF ITS BUILDING AT DORNACH

Lecture given at Liestal, Basle, 11th January 1916

If I try to put forward this evening something about so-called spiritual science, about the way in which it is to be cultivated in the building in Dornach with which you are acquainted, and about that building itself, it is in no way my intention to proselytize or arouse feeling either for spiritual science or for this building.

I have especially in view to speak about certain misunderstandings which are known to exist as regards the aims of the Anthroposophical Society. I will begin with the way in which a more or less unknown thing is judged when it makes its appearance anywhere. It is very easy to understand that anyone unfamiliar with a subject sees in its name something by means of which he thinks he can understand it. Anthroposophy and the Anthroposophical Society are names which have become more widely known than they formerly were through the building in Dornach. 'Anthroposophy' is by no means a new name. When some years ago there was a question of giving our cause a name, I thought of one which had become dear to me because a Professor of Philosophy, Robert Zimmermann,[1] whose lectures I heard in my youth, called his chief work *Anthroposophy*. This was in the eighties of the nineteenth century. Moreover, the name 'Anthroposophy' takes us still further back in literary usage. It was already used in the eighteenth century, indeed, still earlier. The name, therefore, is an old one; we are applying it to something new. For us it does not mean 'human knowledge'. That would be what those who coined the name have in mind. Our science itself leads us to the conviction that within the physical human being there lives a spiritual, inner one — as it were, a second man.

Whereas what man can learn about the world through his senses and through the intellect which relies upon sense-observation may be called 'anthropology', what the spiritual man within us can know may be called 'Anthroposophy'.

Anthroposophy is therefore the knowledge of spiritual man, and that knowledge is not confined to man but is a knowledge of everything which spiritual man can perceive in the spiritual world, just as physical man observes physical things in the world. Because this second, or inner, man is the spiritual man, the knowledge which he acquires may likewise be called 'spiritual science'. And this name is even less new than the name 'Anthroposophy'. That is to say, it is not even unusual, and it would be a complete misunderstanding if anyone were to think that I, as has been said, or anyone closely connected with me, had coined the name 'spiritual science'. The name is used everywhere where it is thought possible to attain knowledge which is not merely physical science but knowledge of something spiritual. Many of our contemporaries call history a spiritual science, call sociology, political economy, aesthetics, and the philosophy of religion spiritual sciences. We use the name in a somewhat different sense, that is, in the sense that spirit is to us something real and actual, whereas most of those who nowadays speak of history, political economy, etc., as spiritual sciences, resolve the spirit into abstract ideas.

I now wish to say something about the development of our Anthroposophical Society, because errors have been circulated on the subject. For instance, it is said that our Anthroposophical Society is only a kind of development out of what is called the 'Theosophical Society'. Although it is true that what we aim at within our Anthroposophical Society found its place for a time within the framework of the general Theosophical Society, yet our Anthroposophical Society must on no account be confused with the Theosophical Society. And in order to prevent this, I must bring forward something — apparently personal — about the gradual emergence of the Anthroposophical Society.

It was about fifteen years ago that I was invited by a small circle of people to give some lectures on spiritual science. These lectures were afterwards published under the title *Mysticism at the Dawn of the Modern Age*[2]. Until then I had, I may say, endeavoured as a solitary thinker to build up a view of the world which on the one hand fully reckons with the great, momentous achievements of the physical sciences, and on the other hand aspires to gain insight into spiritual worlds.

I must emphasize the fact that at the time when I was invited to speak to a small circle in Germany on the subject connected with spiritual science already mentioned, I did not depend in any way upon the works of Blavatsky[3] or of Annie Besant[4], nor did I take them particularly into consideration. The outlook expressed by these books had little in common with my view of the world. I had at that time endeavoured, purely out of what I had discovered for myself, to present some points of view about the spiritual worlds. The lectures were printed; some of them were very soon translated into English, and that by a distinguished member of the Theosophical Society, which at that time was particularly flourishing in England; and from this quarter I was urged to enter the Theosophical Society. At no time had I had any idea, if the occasion should have presented itself in the Theosophical Society, of bringing forward anything save what was built up on the foundation of my own, independent method of research.

That which now forms the substance of our anthroposophical view of the world, as studied in our circle of members, is not borrowed from the Theosophical Society but was represented by me as something entirely independent which — as a result of that Society's invitation — took place within it, until it was found to be heretical and was 'shown the door'; and what had thus always been an independent part of that Society was further developed and cultivated in the now wholly independent Anthroposophical Society.

Thus it is an entirely erroneous conception to confuse in any way what is living within the Anthroposophical Society with what is represented by Blavatsky and Besant. It is true that Blavatsky has in her books put forward important truths concerning spiritual worlds, but mixed with so much error that only one who has accurately investigated these matters can succeed in separating what is significant from what is erroneous. Hence our Anthroposophical Movement must claim to be considered wholly independent. This is not put forward from want of modesty, but merely in order to place a fact in its objectively correct light.

Then came the time when it became necessary to present what our spiritual science, our Anthroposophy, gave in its teachings in the form of dramatic art. We began doing this in 1909 in Munich. From that time onward until 1913 we tried every year, in the dramatic presentations in Munich,[5] to give artistic expression to what our research leads us to acknowledge is living in the world as spiritual forces, as spiritual beings.

These dramatic performances were at first given in an ordinary theatre. But it soon became evident that an ordinary theatre cannot provide the right framework for what was essentially to be a new impulse in the spiritual evolution of mankind. And thus the necessity arose for having a building of our own for such productions, and for the pursuing of our spiritual science and the art arising from it — a building which, moreover, in its form of architecture is an expression of what is intended there. At first it was thought that it would be good to erect such a building in Munich. When this proved impossible or, at any rate, extremely difficult, the possibility arose of erecting this building in Dornach near Basle, on a very beautiful hill, where a large piece of land was offered us by a Swiss friend, who had this ground at his disposal and who has our cause at heart. And thus, through easily comprehensible circumstances, it has come about that this building has been erected in the northwestern corner of Switzerland.

And now, before speaking further about the Dornach building, I should like to deal with the mission of spiritual science itself. It may be quite easy to understand that spiritual science or Anthroposophy, in the sense here intended, is misunderstood. Anyone who has become conversant with this spiritual science finds it entirely comprehensible that many misunderstandings should be brought against it; and one who knows the course taken by the spiritual development of mankind will not be surprised at such misunderstandings. Opinions such as: It is mere fantasy, idle dreaming — or perhaps even worse — are perfectly possible to comprehend. Such things as have entered in this sort of way into mankind's spiritual evolution have generally had a reception similar to that of spiritual science. Moreover, it may very easily appear as if this spiritual science resembled certain older philosophies which are not exactly popular at the present time. If the objectives of spiritual science or Anthroposophy are looked at merely from the outside it may be thought that they resemble those pursued by the Gnostics in the early Christian centuries. But anyone who really learns what our spiritual science is will find that it bears no more resemblance to the Gnosis than does the natural science of the present day to the natural science of the eighth or the sixth century AD. True, resemblances may be found between all possible things, if only a sufficient number of their distinguishing features be eliminated. It may, for instance, be said: This spiritual science, this Anthroposophy, desires to know the world in a spiritual way. The Gnostics also desired to know the world in a spiritual way. Consequently ,spiritual science and Gnosis are one and the same.

In a similar manner, Anthroposophy may be lumped together with, let us say, alchemy, with the magic of the Middle Ages. But this is all due to a complete misapprehension, a complete failure to appreciate the real aims of spiritual science or Anthroposophy. In order to gain insight into this matter, it is necessary to look first at the modern method of thought in natural science, which for three or four centuries has been developing out of quite a different method of thought. It is necessary to realize what it meant for mankind when three or four centuries ago the revolution took place which may be expressed in the words: Up to that time everyone, learned and ignorant alike, believed that the Earth stood still in the midst of the universe, and that the Sun and stars revolved around the Earth. It may be said that in consequence of what Copernicus, Galileo, and others taught at that time, the ground under men's feet was made mobile. But when the movement of the Earth is looked upon as a matter of course, there is no feeling left of the surprising effect produced upon humanity by this and everything connected with it.

Now what natural science sought to do then for the interpretation and explanation of the mysteries of nature, spiritual science seeks to do for the spirit and soul at the present time. Fundamentally speaking, spiritual science desires quite simply to be something similar for the life of soul and spirit to what natural science became at that time for the life of outer nature. Anyone who believes, for instance, that our spiritual science has something to do with the ancient Gnosis completely ignores the fact that something new entered the mental evolution of mankind with the view of the world adopted by natural science, and that as a result of this new element spiritual science is to be something similarly new for the investigation of spiritual worlds.

Now if spiritual science is to do the same for spirit that natural science has done for nature, it must investigate quite differently from the latter. It must find ways and means of penetrating into the sphere of the spiritual, a domain which cannot be perceived with outer physical senses, nor apprehended with the intellect which is bound to the brain.

It is still difficult to speak intelligibly about the ways and means found by spiritual science for penetrating into the spiritual sphere, because the spiritual world is generally considered, from the outset, as something unknown — indeed, as something which must necessarily remain unknown. Now spiritual science shows that the cognitive powers which man has in ordinary life, and which he also uses in ordinary science, are by no means able to penetrate into the spiritual world. In this respect spiritual science is in full accord with certain branches of natural science. But natural science is unaware that there slumber in man certain faculties which are capable of being developed.

It is, again, difficult to speak of these faculties at the present time, for the reason that they are very widely confused with all manner of diseased phenomena in mankind. For instance, there is much talk nowadays of the possibility of the acquiring of certain abnormal faculties, and the natural scientist thereupon declares that it is true that they may be acquired but that their existence is only due to the fact that the otherwise normal nervous system and brain have become abnormal and diseased. In every case in which the investigator in natural science is correct in making such a statement, the spiritual investigator at once acknowledges it. But the aims of spiritual science should not be confused with what is often superficially called 'clairvoyance'. Neither should spiritual science be confused with what appears under the name of spiritualism and the like. The essential thing is this, that spiritual science should be distinguished from everything that is in any way due to diseased human predispositions.

In order to make myself quite clear on this point, I must indicate, if only in a few words, the manner in which the spiritual investigator conducts his researches. The method of research in spiritual science is founded on something which has nothing to do with the soul-forces of man in so far as they are bound up with his bodily organism. If, for instance, it is said that spiritual science is founded on what is to be attained through some form of asceticism, or on something for which the nervous system is prepared and stimulated in a certain way, or that it results from the bringing of spirits into manifestation in an outer physical way — all such assertions would be utterly inaccurate. What the spiritual investigator has to do to acquire the faculty of looking into the spiritual world consists exclusively of processes of spirit and soul; they have nothing to do with changes in the body, nor with visions arising from an abnormal bodily life.

The spiritual investigator will be most careful not to let the body have any influence over what he spiritually perceives. I mention by the way that if, for instance, a large number of the adherents of spiritual science are vegetarians, this is a matter of taste, which in principle has nothing to do with spiritual methods of research. It has only to do with making life a little easier, with a more comfortable ordering of one's life, since it is easier to work in a spiritual way if no meat is eaten.

The main point is that spiritual science, with its methods of research, only begins where modern natural science leaves off. Humanity is indebted to the view of the world adopted by natural science for what I would call a logic which educates itself by the facts of nature. An important method of training has been introduced, amongst those who have concerned themselves with natural science, with regard to the inner application of thinking. I will now try to make clear by a comparison the relation of spiritual-scientific research to that of natural science. The mode of thought used by the researcher in natural science I would compare with the forms of a statue. The logic developed from the outer facts of nature has something lifeless in it. When we think logically, we have images in our conceptions and ideas. But these images are only inner thought-forms, just as the forms of a statue are forms.

Now the spiritual investigator sets out from this mode of thinking. In my book, *Knowledge of the Higher Worlds. How is it Achieved?*, directions are to be found as to what must be done with thinking in order that it may become something entirely different from what it is in ordinary life and ordinary science. The spiritual investigator develops his thinking, he makes it undergo a certain special discipline. I cannot in this short sketch enter into details, which are given in the book to which I have referred. When thinking, when the logic that holds sway in man, is applied in a certain way, the whole inner life of the soul is changed. Something happens which changes this soul-life into something other than what it is, which I will once more make clear by a comparison.

Imagine that the statue — this, of course, cannot happen, but let us assume that it could — imagine that the statue, which previously stood there with its lifeless form, were suddenly to begin to walk and to become living. This the statue cannot do; but human thinking, inner logical activity, can. By means of the soul-exercises undertaken and carried out by the spiritual investigator, his condition becomes such that there is within him not only a thought-out logic, but a living logic; logic itself becomes a living being within him. In this way he has grasped something which lives and surges within him, permeating his whole being; and this takes the place of dead concepts. And when spiritual research assumes the existence of an etheric body in addition to the physical body which is visible to bodily eyes, by this is meant not something merely imagined, but rather that man, by bringing life to logical thinking, becomes conscious of a second man within him. This is a matter of experience which may be arrived at. The experience must be made in order that the science of the spiritual man may arise, just as the outer experiments of natural science must be made in order to learn nature's secrets.

Just as thinking is so transformed that it no longer leads merely to images but becomes inwardly active and alive, so may the will also be developed in a certain way. The methods by which the will is so cultivated that we learn to know it as something different from what it is in ordinary life are also to be found in the book referred to above. Through this development of the will something of a quite different kind results from what comes through the development of thinking. If we desire to do something in ordinary life, if we work, the will penetrates, as it were, into the limbs. We say, 'I will', and move our hands; but the will comes to expression only in this movement. In its real essence it remains unknown. But by using certain exercises the will may be released from its connection with the limbs. The will may be experienced in itself alone. Thinking may be made active, so as to become something inwardly alive, a kind of etheric body. The will can be stripped bare, separated from its connection with the bodily nature, and then we become aware — in a far higher sense than is the case with thinking — that we have a second man within us, who has a consciousness of his own. If we work upon our will in the necessary way, something takes place which I can only make clear by reminding you that in ordinary human life there are two alternating states, waking life and sleep. In waking life man lives consciously; during sleep, consciousness ceases.

Now at first it is a mere assertion to say that the soul and spirit do not fall into abeyance between the time of falling asleep and awaking. But they are no longer directly in the body: they are outside it. The spiritual investigator succeeds in voluntarily giving his bodily life the same form that it takes involuntarily when he goes to sleep. He commands his senses and his ordinary intellect to be still; he achieves this by developing his will. And it then happens that the same condition is voluntarily brought about that is usually involuntarily present in sleep. Yet, on the other hand, what is now brought about is the complete opposite of the condition of sleep. Whereas during sleep we become unconscious and know nothing about ourselves and our surroundings, through developing the will in the manner described we consciously leave our bodies; we see the body outside ourselves, just as we usually perceive an external object outside ourselves. Then we notice that in man there lives a real spectator of his thoughts and actions. This is no mere image, no merely pictorial expression; it is a reality. In our will there lives something which is perpetually observing us inwardly. It is easy to look upon this inner spectator as something intended to be taken pictorially; the spiritual investigator knows it to be a reality, just as sense-perceptible objects are realities. And if we have these two, the etheric man, who thinks in living, moving thoughts, and this inner spectator, then we have brought ourselves into a spiritual world which is actually experienced, just as the physical world is experienced with the senses. In this way we discover a second man within us, just as oxygen is found in water by the methods of natural science.

What is attained by a developed thinking is not visions but spiritual sight of realities; what is attained by a developed will is not ordinary soul-experiences, but the discovery of a consciousness different from the ordinary. There now act upon one another those aspects of our nature which are, logic in motion and what is represented as a higher consciousness. If we come to know these two within us, we know that part of man which exists even when his physical body falls into decay, when he goes through the gate of death. We come to know that aspect of man's being which does not act through the outer body, which is of a soul and spirit nature, which will continue to exist after death, which existed also before birth, or, let us say, before conception. We learn to know the eternal aspect of man's being, forming it as it were out of our ordinary mortal human nature, just as we can separate oxygen out of water by a chemical process.

All that I have now brought before you will inevitably still be looked upon as fantastic at the present time; in relation to customary ideas it is as fantastic as the words of Copernicus seemed, when he said: 'It is not the Sun which revolves around the Earth, but the Earth which revolves around the Sun.' Nevertheless, what appears so fantastic is really only something unfamiliar. It is not the case that something invented or dreamed up has been related in what has just been set forth, but the point is that the spiritual actually comes to be regarded as a fact through inner experiences. The spiritual investigator is not speaking in a simple manner of man's nature when he says that man consists of a physical body, etheric body, astral body, etc., but he is showing how human nature, when it is contemplated as a whole, becomes split up into the particular members of which it is composed. And if the matter be regarded in accordance with its fundamental essence, nothing magical or mystical in a bad sense is meant by these members of man's being. Spiritual science shows that man consists of different gradations, different shades of human nature. And this in a higher sphere is no different from the fact, in a lower one, that light may be so experimented with as to appear in seven colours. Just as light must be split up into seven colours in order that it may be studied, so must man be divided into his several parts that he may be properly contemplated.

It should not be expected that what is spiritual can be brought before the eyes, before the senses. It must be experienced inwardly and spiritually. And anyone who will not admit that inner experience — spiritual experience — is in any way a fact will consider anything that is said by the spiritual investigator to be mere empty skirmishing with words. To one who becomes acquainted with spiritual facts, these are realities in a far higher sense than are physical facts. If a plant grows and develops blossom and fruit, a new plant develops out of the seed; and if we have come to know the germ, we see that it has the full force of the plant within it and that a new plant arises from the germ.

What is of the nature of spirit and soul must be gleaned from facts belonging to the spirit and soul; we shall then know that in the living thinking which is liberated from the will, a life-germ has been discerned which passes through the gate of death, goes through the spiritual world after death and afterwards returns again to earthly life. And just as surely as the plant-seed develops a new plant, so does the kernel of man's being develop a new earthly life. This new aspect can be seen in what is now before us, for this becomes inwardly alive.

Natural science has methods of calculating certain events which will happen in the future. From the relative positions of the Sun and Moon it may be calculated when eclipses of these will occur. It is only necessary to know the corresponding factors in order to calculate when a certain constellation of the stars will become manifest. In these cases it is necessary to use mathematics, because we are dealing with external space. But what we inwardly experience as the life-germ also points in a living way towards future earthly lives. Just as future eclipses of the Sun and Moon are indicated in the present relations of those bodies, so are future earthly lives indicated in what now lives within us. In this case we are not dealing with what is called — according to more ancient views — the transmigration of souls, but with something which modern spiritual research discovers from the facts of spiritual life, which are capable of being investigated.

Now certain things must be carefully kept in view if we wish to understand the real foundations of spiritual research. We succeed in enabling our soul and spirit nature to leave the body through working with thinking and will in the manner that has been indicated. We are then outside the body; and just as we usually have outer things before our eyes, so do we have our physical body before us. But the essential thing is that we can always observe this body. And if it is a case of spiritual research in the true sense of the words, as is here meant, what takes place in a diseased soul-life must never be allowed to occur. For what is the characteristic feature of an abnormal or diseased soul-life? If someone is put into a hypnotic state or so-called trance, as certain conditions are called, and speaks out of the subconscious, which is often referred to as a kind of clairvoyance, the essential point is that the ordinary consciousness is not present whilst the changed consciousness is in control. The former has been transformed into a dulled, abnormal consciousness. It will never be possible to say, when observing an unhealthy condition of soul, that the healthy soul-person would certainly not be unhealthy or abnormal.

In real spiritual research the fact is that an individual arrives at a changed consciousness, but that as a normal human being he is all the time standing by. The condition that is proper to the spiritual investigator is not developed *from out of* ordinary normal soul-life but *alongside* it. In the case of a genuine spiritual investigator, he lives, during his researches, outside his body; but his body continues to work on undisturbed together with all his normal soul-functions and his ordinary intellect, which remains completely normal. The individual concerned, if he is a true spiritual investigator, remains a normal human being, in spite of the fact that he has left his body, together with what he has developed within himself; and one who cannot himself investigate spiritually really need not see that the other is living in a different world. The non-hypnotized person is not present beside the hypnotized one, the person with a normal soul-life is not present beside the one who is developing an abnormal soul-life. But the characteristic feature of spiritual research is that while it is being pursued the person's normal condition is completely maintained. Precisely on this account is the spiritual investigator in a position accurately to distinguish true spiritual research from what appears in any diseased conditions of soul.

Another mistake arises when it is thought that spiritual research has anything in common with spiritualism. By this it is not meant that all manner of facts may not be discovered through spiritualism, but these belong to natural science, not to spiritual science; for what is discovered through spiritualism is presented to the outer senses, whether by means of materializations, or knockings and the like. What can be presented to the senses belongs to natural science. What offers itself as an object to the spiritual investigator is of a soul and spirit nature, and cannot be presented externally, for instance, in space; it must be experienced inwardly.

Through the inner experience which has been described there is formed a comprehensive spiritual science, which not only throws light on the being of man and the passage through repeated earthly lives, but also illuminates the spiritual worlds and the spiritual beings who lie behind nature. Spiritual research is able to enter the world through which man passes after death. But it must not be thought that what appear in ordinary life as abnormal faculties have any special value in spiritual science. There is much talk nowadays of the possibility of telepathy. We will not now enter into all the pros and cons of this matter. People must grow accustomed to many things in the course of time. Precisely at the present time serious investigators are wrestling with the problem of the divining-rod, which is now so widely used, and about which one of the most down-to-earth of investigators is currently making important experiments in order to ascertain what influence a person is under who is successful with the divining-rod. But all this belongs to the department of finer natural science. Similarly, the idea that thoughts entertained by one person are able to influence another at a distance also belongs to this department. True spiritual research cannot use such forces for gaining knowledge about the world of soul and spirit. It is a complete misunderstanding of spiritual science to think that it looks upon the teaching about telepathy as anything other than a part of a refined physiology, a refined form of natural science.

The spiritual-scientific manner of research must not be confused with what appears nowadays as spiritualism. When spiritual science remembers the human souls which are passing through a purely spiritual life in a spiritual world between death and rebirth, it knows that these souls are living purely in a soul-condition in the spiritual world. Now it is possible for the spirit and soul that is in a human body to turn to the dead in such a way that a real connection is made with them. But this turning to the dead must itself be of a purely soul-spiritual character. Spiritual science shows this. And the directing of our own soul-life to our beloved dead may acquire deep significance, even while we ourselves are still in the physical world. It cannot be at variance with any religious belief if, through the view of the world taken by spiritual science, remembrance of the dead and active communion with them is cultivated in this way, if spiritual science stimulates this living together with the dead. In this connection it must always be borne in mind that the dead person can only be aware of our solicitude for him if he desires such a connection with us. This is also shown by spiritual science. The exercise of any power over the dead is entirely remote from the intentions of the spiritual investigator. He knows quite well that the dead are living in a sphere in which the circumstances of the will are different from those in the physical world; and if he were to wish to penetrate into the spiritual world, taking with him what he is able to develop here within the physical world, it would seem to him as though — to use a comparison — a company of people were sitting here and a lion suddenly appeared through the floor and caused havoc. Similar havoc would result if an earthly human being were to force his way into the life of the dead in an unbefitting manner. Therefore there can be no question in spiritual science of summoning the dead, in the way in which this is attempted in spiritualism, for the very reason that the relations of the living to the dead are illuminated in a wonderful way by what spiritual science arouses in our souls. And since amongst the numerous errors which have been urged against our spiritual science there is the idea that with regard to the dead it has a connection with spiritualism, it is necessary to emphasize very sharply that this is a misunderstanding. Nothing less than the absolute contrary of the truth is asserted with regard to spiritual science in this matter.

As already said, I do not wish to proselytize or arouse feelings for our cause, but only to mention misunderstandings which I know to be prevalent, and to indicate in the clearest way possible the relation of spiritual science to these matters.

Now the question is also asked — and it is even considered a rather obvious one — as to how spiritual science or Anthroposophy stands in relation to the religious life of man. Its very nature, however, altogether prevents it from intervening directly in any religious confession, in any sphere of religious life. In this connection I can perhaps make myself clear in the following way. Let us assume that our concern is with natural science. Because we gain a knowledge of nature, we do not imagine that we are able to create something in nature itself. Knowledge of nature does not create anything in nature. Nor, because we gain knowledge of spiritual conditions, shall we imagine that we are able to create something in the world of spirit. We observe spiritual circumstances. Spiritual science endeavours to penetrate behind the mysteries of the spiritual circumstances in the world. Religions are facts in the historical life of humanity. Spiritual science can, of course, go so far as to consider the spiritual phenomena which have appeared as religions in the course of the world's evolution. But spiritual science can never desire to create a religion, any more than natural science surrenders itself to the illusion of being able to create something in nature. Hence the most various religious confessions will be able to live together in the profoundest peace and in complete harmony within the circle of the anthroposophical view of the world, and will be able to strive together after knowledge of the spiritual — so to strive that the religious convictions of the individual will not thereby be in any way encroached upon. Neither need intensity in the exercise of a religious belief or in attending services be in any way lessened by what is found in spiritual science. Rather must it be said that natural science, as it has appeared in modern times, has very often led people away from a religious conception of life, from the exercise of true, inner religion. It is an experience which we have in connection with spiritual science that people who have been alienated from all religious life by the half truths of natural science can be brought back again to that life through spiritual science. No one need be in any way estranged from his religious life through spiritual science. For this reason it cannot be said that spiritual science, as such, is a religious belief. It desires neither to create a religious belief, nor to change an individual in any way with regard to the religious belief which he holds. Nevertheless, it seems as though people were talking about the religion of the anthroposophists! In reality such a thing cannot be said, for all religious beliefs are represented within the Anthroposophical Society; and no one is prevented by it in a practical sense from exercising his religious belief in the fullest, most comprehensive and most intense way. Spiritual science seeks to include the whole world in its survey; it seeks also to survey historical life, taking into account the lofty spiritual initiatives which have entered the stream of history. That for this reason it also undertakes a survey of religions is absolutely no contradiction of what I have just said. And thus it is that the spiritual-scientific view of the world adds a certain depth to a person's experience, as also with regard to the objectives of religious life.

But when, for instance, it happens that spiritual science is accused of not speaking of a personal God, when it is said that I prefer to speak of the Godhead, not of God, when it is asserted that what is called 'the divine' in spiritual science is of a similar nature to what is so designated in the pantheism of the Monists or Naturalists — this is the complete opposite of the truth. Through the very circumstance that in spiritual science we are led to real spiritual beings and to the real being that man is after death, just because we are led to concrete, real spiritual beings, we arrive at being able completely to understand how absurd it is to become a pantheist, how nonsensical to deny personality in God: On the contrary, one comes to see that one may speak not only of the personality, but even of a super-personality of God.

The most thorough refutation of pantheism may be found through spiritual science.

Can it be a subject of reproach that the spiritual investigator speaks with only the deepest reverence when, out of the feeling which his knowledge arouses in him, he points the way with awe to the divine? How often it is said in the circle of our friends: 'In Him we live and move and have our being.' And anyone who seeks to comprehend God with a single idea does not know that all possible ideas cannot comprehend God, because all ideas are in God. But the recognition of God as a being who has personality in a much higher sense even than man, in a sense which even through spiritual science cannot be fully perceived, becomes, I would say, quite natural to people especially through Anthroposophy. Religious conceptions are not made hazy, in a pantheistic sense, through spiritual science, but become deepened in accordance with their nature. If we say that God is revealed in our own hearts and souls, this is surely the conviction of many religious people; and it is again and again said in spiritual science that there can be no question in this of wishing to deify man.

I have often used the simile that a drop taken out of the sea is water — do I therefore say that the drop is the sea? If I say that something divine speaks in the individual human soul, a drop out of the ocean of the infinite divine, do I therefore say anything which deifies the individual human soul? Do I say anything which unites nature with God in a pantheistic way? Far from it. And finally, if from certain deeply-seated feelings which are aroused by spiritual science itself, the name of God is, in reverential awe, not referred to directly but paraphrased, should this be a subject of blame from the religious point of view? I ask, is not one of the Ten Commandments, 'Thou shalt not take the name of the Lord thy God in vain?'. Might not spiritual science be contributing towards a faithful fulfilment of this command if the name of God is not perpetually on the lips of its followers?

And the Name and Being of Christ? It is precisely of spiritual science that it may be said that it makes every effort to understand the Being of Christ, and that in doing so it is never at variance with what is developed, from true foundations, by any religious denomination. In this very domain, however, we meet with something most singular. Someone comes and says he has a certain conception or feeling about Christ, about Jesus, and we say to him, 'Certainly, these feelings can be seen as wholly justified; but spiritual science leads to thinking many other things about Christ as well. It does not deny what you say, but accepts it. But it adds much more to it.'

Just because spiritual science widens the spiritual sight, the eye of the soul, to extend over the spiritual world, it is necessary not only to recognize in the Being to whom the Christian looks up as his Christ, the one who walked this Earth, but to bring this Being into connection with the entire cosmos. And there is much else which results from this. But nothing which results from it takes anything away from the knowledge of Christ; rather is something added to what a religious person, a truly Christian religious person, has to say about the Christ. And when someone attacks the conception of Christ Jesus held by spiritual science, it always seems to the spiritual investigator as though someone comes and says, 'I have this or that to say about the Christ; do you believe it?' 'Yes!' we say. 'Yet you do not merely believe this but more besides!'. This he will not allow. He is not satisfied with our admitting what he advocates and forbids us to declare something still greater and grander about the Christ than he himself declares.

For can it really be a heresy when spiritual science, out of its very foundations, out of its perception of what, as spirit, permeates the entire progress of the Earth with regard to human and other evolution, concludes that the whole existence of the Earth would have no significance for the universe if the Mystery of Golgotha had not taken place within the earthly sphere? The spiritual investigator must say: 'If any inhabitants of distant worlds were to look down upon the Earth and see what it is, they would see no meaning in the whole evolution of the Earth unless Christ had lived, died and risen again upon it. The event of Golgotha gives meaning and purpose to earthly life for the whole world. If you were to study the results of spiritual research, you would see that reverence for Christ and devotion to Him cannot be diminished by such research, but on the contrary can only be enhanced.'

Time presses, and I cannot enter into many other misunderstandings which have been spread abroad concerning certain thoughts about the Bible which are said to be prevalent in circles of anthroposophists, as they are called — although the word would be better avoided, and only 'Anthroposophy' used. The point in this case is that a person may be a very good spiritual investigator without in any way being able to accept what has, for definite reasons, been said for these sections of our Society where there is such a wish to know something about the Gospels or the Bible generally. But if what is said be read within its context, it will be found that, for instance, I never uttered such nonsense as that repeated earthly lives could be proved from the Bible by means of the passage in which Nathanael is spoken of. It has been asserted that I thought that when the Christ says, 'When you were under the fig-tree, I saw you,' he is referring to an earlier incarnation, in which he saw Nathanael sitting under the fig-tree. I can do but one thing when these misunderstandings fly about the world today. I can do but one thing — wonder how such things have been able to arise at all out of what was really said. They are just proofs of the manner in which what is really said becomes altered in the most diverse ways when it is repeated from one person to another, and how the contrary — for in this case it is the contrary that emerged — of what I had said was attributed to me.

I will not now discuss other misunderstandings, which could easily be refuted. I shall confine myself to one, which could be expressed as follows: What do you think of the fact that nothing about repeated earthly lives is found in the Bible? It might be that someone would say that he could not believe in repeated earthly lives, for the simple reason that, according to his convictions, there is a contradiction between accepting the idea of repeated earthly lives — although minds such as Lessing's, for instance, admitted it as true — and what is in the Bible.

Now repeated earthly lives will come to be accepted as a scientific, a spiritual-scientific, fact, and people will learn to think in the following way about the relation to the Bible of such a fact of spiritual science, which had sooner or later to be discovered. Would it be thought possible for anyone to say he did not believe in the existence of America because the Bible does not mention such a place? Or would it be thought offensive to the Bible to say: 'I think the existence of America is quite in harmony with my reverence for the Bible, in spite of its omission of any mention of America?' Is there anything in the Bible about the truth of the Copernican view of the universe? There have been people who for this reason have looked upon the Copernican view of the world as something false and forbidden. Nowadays there is no one really versed in the culture of his time who could say that he found a contradiction between the teaching of Copernicus and the Bible — notwithstanding that the teaching of Copernicus is not in the Bible.

In the same way it may be said of the spiritual-scientific fact of repeated earthly lives that nothing is done to prejudice recognition of the cardinal truths of the Bible merely because nothing can be found therein about reincarnation and because, indeed, much of its content may be so interpreted as to seem to contradict this knowledge. These points must, however, be looked at from the right point of view. If they are so looked at, it may very well be remembered how such things change in the course of time. If someone says he will not admit the truth of repeated earthly lives for the reason that it contradicts the Bible, I am always reminded that there was a time when Galileo was treated — as is well known — in a very peculiar way, because he had something to say which, apparently — but only apparently — contradicted the Bible. Or we may remember how Giordano Bruno was treated, because he too had something to say about which it was asserted that it could not be verified from the Bible.

I also remember a priest from the theological faculty who became the rector of a university some years ago and who in his rectorial address, the subject of which was Galileo, spoke as a Catholic priest somewhat as follows. He said that times change, and with them the way in which people accept recognized facts. Galileo was in his time treated in the way we all know; but now every true Christian sees that through the discovery of the grandeur of the cosmic system, as it became known through Galileo, the glory and majesty of God and devotion to Him can only be increased, not diminished. This was a truly priestly, a truly Christian, thing to say — indeed it was perhaps said for the first time in a really Christian way. And the fine recognition of Galileo, which sounded through the entire address of this priest, was also Christian.

On the whole I would say, speaking from the convictions of spiritual science, that the spiritual scientist must, through his teachings, so think of what Christianity is, and of what Christ is to the world, as to say: 'How faint-hearted are those who think that in consequence of some discovery in the physical or spiritual domain the greatness which breathes towards us from the revelation of Christ can be diminished.' To the spiritual investigator a person who thinks that through some fact — even such a weighty one as repeated earthly lives — which is discovered in the physical or spiritual sphere, the splendour of the Christ-event and the influence of Christ can be diminished for the Christian, seems faint-hearted — anyone who believes this might also believe that the Sun loses power because it does not shine only for Europe but for America too.

Whatever further physical or spiritual facts may be discovered, in any far-distant future, the great truths of Christianity will outshine them all. This is discerned by anyone who approaches the Christ-impulse and the entire Christian conception of the world with the attitude of spiritual research. Such a person is not so faint-hearted as to say that the splendour of Christianity can be diminished by any investigation. He knows that anyone who believes that Christianity can be imperilled by any physical or spiritual research does not think much of Christianity.

It is really a question of whether perhaps the numerous misunderstandings which exist with regard to that for which the Dornach building is an outward sign, an outer home, can be overcome. About the Dornach building itself I will only say today that it is intended to be none other than an artistic embodiment of what is aroused in our perceptions and feelings when we have received into our souls the living essence of spiritual science or Anthroposophy. Therefore it should not be thought that the ideas of spiritual science are pictured by means of symbols or allegories in the forms of the building. Of that there is no question at all.

If you study this building you will find that it has the peculiarity of having nothing at all mysterious in it, not a single symbol, nothing allegorical or the like. This has, from the very nature of the building, been kept entirely remote from it.

It may perhaps be said: But it is necessary to know the thoughts belonging to spiritual science in order to understand what one sees. This is true, but it is what the art of the Dornach building has in common with every other art. Take the Sistine Madonna, the wonderful picture of the Mother with the Jesus child. I think that if a person who had never heard anything about Christianity were to stand before the Sistine Madonna, it would be necessary to explain to him what it is, for he too would not be able to understand the subject out of his own feelings. Thus it is a matter of course that it is necessary to live in the whole stream of spiritual science in order to understand its art, just as it is necessary to be in the midst of Christianity in order to understand the Sistine Madonna.

The attempt is not made, in the Dornach building, to express the ideas of spiritual science symbolically, but underlying it is the idea that spiritual science is something — and this follows from what I have said here today — which takes hold of man's inner being in such a living, powerful way that faculties otherwise dormant in him — artistic faculties as well as others — are awakened. And as spiritual science is something new — not a new name for something old, but something really new — just as present-day natural science is new as compared with the science of the Middle Ages, its art too must be something new and different from existing works of art. Gothic art represented a new departure from the art of antiquity; anyone who is of the opinion that only the art of antiquity is of value may revile Gothic art. Similarly, a new style arising out of a new way of feeling may also be disparaged.

A certain utility building is regarded as particularly bad. Near the building with two domes stands a boiler house. The attempt has been made artistically to construct a useful building out of the most modern of materials: concrete. The concrete was taken into account. If anyone explains the form allegorically, if he sees all kinds of symbols in it, he is just a dreamer, a visionary, not one who sees what is there. Just as a nutshell is shaped so as to fit the kernel, so does the artist try, in what he constructs, to form a shell for what is within it, a shell in conformity with nature, so that the outer form is the appropriate covering for what it contains. That is what is attempted. And the point of view of someone who criticizes this building and does not find it beautiful can be understood, for one must first grow used to these things. But he might perhaps try to imagine another chimney, as chimneys are now built, beside our boiler house, a proper, red chimney with the building that goes with it; and he might then compare the two.

To be sure, we very well know that what is being attempted in the building at Dornach is but a beginning, and an imperfect beginning, but it is intended as the beginning of a new style of architecture which is arising out of a new view of the world. There are also people who have said: Look, you have made seven columns, seven on each side of the main hall. You are a very superstitious society; you believe in the mystical number seven.

Well, a person who sees seven colours in the rainbow might also be thought superstitious. In that case it is really nature which should be thought superstitious, for it is responsible for this. But anyone who talks about these seven columns should not at first dwell on the number, but consider what has been newly attempted in the matter. It is generally always the case that similar columns are placed next to one another. The capitals of our columns are conceived as a continuous series; the second column is different from the first, the third again different; one capital arises out of another. This results in an organism which has inner laws in the same way as have the seven tones from the tonic to the seventh.

It will thus be found that nowhere has anything been done out of ideas, symbolism, or the realm of mystery; the endeavour has rather everywhere been made to develop something artistic in forms, colours and so forth. We have striven to make the whole building the right framework for what is to be carried on within it. Buildings have walls. In walls, as they have hitherto been built, people are accustomed to see something so formed as to enclose a space. Our walls are clothed internally with forms to such an extent that there is no feeling of space being enclosed by the form but one has the feeling that the wall is transparent and that one is looking out into the infinite. The walls are so moulded in their forms that it is as though they were not really there, and we remain in connection with nature and the whole world.

In this short account I have not sought to convince anyone. I wished to do only what I laid stress on at the beginning; I wish to awaken interest rather than to convince. But one thing I should like to emphasize once more: the way in which people become conversant with a particular view of the world depends on their habits of thought. And anyone who is acquainted with the course taken by the spiritual evolution of mankind knows that truth has always had to unfold through obstacles. Just consider how Giordano Bruno had to appear before humanity,[6] a humanity which had always believed that the blue vault of heaven was the limit of space. Giordano Bruno had to tell people: There is nothing at all where you see the blue vault of the sky; you put something there yourselves when you look at it. Space stretches out into infinity, and infinite worlds are in the infinite space. What Giordano Bruno then did for physical observation, spiritual science has to do for soul and spirit, and for the dimension of time. In regard to soul and spirit there is also a kind of firmament; on one side, birth — or let us say conception — on the other side, death. But that firmament is actually just as little a reality as the blue firmament above; merely because people can only see as far as birth or conception and as far as death with ordinary human faculties of perception, they think there is a boundary there, as people used to think the firmament was a boundary. But just as the blue firmament is no boundary but, rather, represents infinite worlds existing in infinite space, so must we, with extended faculties, look out beyond the firmament of birth and death into an infinity of time, and behold in it the development of the eternal soul throughout successive earthly lives. In the spiritual sphere things are not different from what they are in the sphere of natural science. Therefore it may be asked: How is it then that so many misunderstandings arise from so many quarters about spiritual science? From my own personal point of view I must say that I think the reasons why spiritual science meets with so much hostility and misunderstanding are partly objective and partly subjective.

Amongst the objective reasons I would place this one first and foremost: spiritual science is something upon which it is necessary to concentrate one's thoughts seriously. Long and earnest work is needed in order to understand it, work which brings with it many experiences and also many disappointments. But this is, in reality, the case with every realm of study. The paths opened up by Anthroposophy cannot be found without such work. It seems to be the custom to say that for the understanding of a watch it is necessary to learn how the wheels synchronize. This demands some trouble. But it does not seem to be equally customary to make a similar admission with regard to the universe as a whole. In this case difficult, apparently complicated, views are not allowed to count, and yet they are only difficult because the subject in question is so. Instead of studying spiritual science themselves, people find fault with it because, judged from their own point of view, it is difficult.

Then there are subjective reasons. And these are to be found in what I have already said. It is difficult for people in general to reconcile ideas which they have once formed with ideas to which they are unaccustomed. Such unaccustomed ideas need not even contradict those already held, but need only add something to what has already been thought.

It has always been thus with truth. What is contradicted is people's habits of thought. And from this point of view, if the subjective reasons for misunderstandings about spiritual science are sought, we must say that the reasons are the same as those which led to the teaching of Copernicus being rejected by the whole world when it first appeared. It was just something new. Truth has to make its own way in the world, though it does so in the end.

Anyone who is involved with spiritual science and with what it is able to bring about will be well aware of this. He relies on the experience that truth always works its way through the smallest crevices in the rocks of prejudices which have become established. Perhaps spiritual science may still be hated now. But anyone who hates it will, at the most, only be able to make others hate it with him, people who are attached to him and swear by what he says. But never yet has a truth been effaced through having been hated. Truth may at any time be misunderstood and misinterpreted, but there will always be found those who know and rightly understand, in the face of those who misconstrue and misjudge. And even if what spiritual science has to say in our time is not now recognized as true, if it is misunderstood and unappreciated, the time will come for this science also. Truth may be suppressed, but not destroyed. It will always be born again, however often it may be suppressed.

For truth is intimately, deeply and vitally bound up with the human soul, in such a way that one may be convinced that the human soul and truth belong to one another like sisters. And even if there are times and places in which dissension comes about between them, and some misunderstanding arises, recognition and mutual love must always reappear between the soul and truth. For they are sisters, who have a common origin, and must always be lovingly mindful of their common origin — their origin in the spirituality which rules throughout the universe and which it is the task of Anthroposophy to explore.

AFTERWORD

The intention has been to show how anthroposophical spiritual
science acquires the knowledge of the spiritual world which gives
it its present form through following paths which can hold their
own beside the established paths of a scientific way of looking at
things. In order to penetrate into the spiritual world in just as
sure a manner as natural science does into the world of matter,
spiritual science must take paths which are different from those of
natural science. In order to satisfy in a spiritual sphere the same
demands which natural science satisfies in its sphere, it must work
with faculties of perception and knowledge which are adapted
to the spiritual, just as those of natural science are adapted to
nature. By the very virtue of the fact that a spiritual science with
aims such as these cannot be confused with older world outlooks
such as, for example, the Gnosis, it can be clearly observed that
there has in recent times been a strong wish to reach towards it.
Therefore it does not come forth as something which is arbitrarily
fabricated at the present time, but rather as the fulfilment of
hopes which can be observed in the cultural development of the
West. Many things might be adduced to prove this, but we will just
give two examples here, which show that 'Anthroposophy' is
something that has been thought about for a long time. Troxler, a
thinker of the first half of the nineteenth century who is much
underestimated, published his *Vorlesungen über Philosophie*
(Lectures on philosophy) in 1835. In this work there is the sentence:
'Although it is highly gratifying that the latest philosophy, which ...
must be revealed in every *anthroposophy* (that is, in poetry as much
as it is in history) — has higher aspirations, we must not overlook
the fact that this idea cannot be the fruit of speculation, and that the
true personality or individuality of man should not be confused
either with what it propounds as subjective spirit or final ego, or
with what it contrasts with this as absolute spirit or absolute
personality.'[7]. What Troxler puts forward regarding this idea of
Anthroposophy is confined to statements which clearly show how
close he is to the acknowledgement that there are in human nature
other members than the physical body. He says: 'In earlier times
philosophers differentiated a delicate, sublime soul-body from the
grosser body. This they considered to be a kind of mantle for the
spirit. They called it the model, and looked upon it as the inner,

higher man.' The connection in which these words are found in Troxler's work, and the whole of his conception of the world, testify that we may see in his case aspirations which are fulfilled in the spiritual science that has been spoken of in the present essay. But as Troxler is not in the position to recognize that Anthroposophy is only possible through the development of soul-capacities along the lines that have been indicated here, his own views relapse to points of view which, as compared with those attained by J. G. Fichte, Schelling and Hegel are not an advance, but a retrogression. (See my book *The Riddles of Philosophy*). In the work of I. H. Fichte, the son of the great philosopher, (in his *Anthropologie*, second edition 1860, p. 608), we find the following sentences: 'Anthropology ends in the result which is confirmed from various quarters, that the true nature of man's being and the real source of his consciousness belong to a supersensible world. But sense-consciousness and the phenomenal world which appears before his eyes, together with the whole of the life of the senses, have no other importance than merely to be the place where that supersensible life of the spirit is enacted, by his bringing the spiritual content of ideas into the sense-perceptible world through his own free, conscious act. ... The final result of this fundamental comprehension of human nature raises "anthropology" to *"Anthroposophy"*.' In connection with the explanation of these sentences I. H. Fichte says (p. 609): 'Thus in the end, Anthroposophy itself is only able to find its final conclusion in Theosophy'. The reasons why I. H. Fichte with his own view of the world did not arrive at Anthroposophy but fell behind J. G. Fichte, Schelling and Hegel, are the same as in Troxler's case. For the present we will only give these two examples out of a multitude of facts contained in the history of the spiritual development of mankind, which could be adduced to prove that the anthroposophical spiritual science characterized in this essay bears a correspondence with a scientific tendency which has existed for a long time.

*

In a lecture which I gave in 1902 before the Giordano Bruno Union,[8] I referred to these statements by I. H. Fichte (which seemed to me to be the expression of a modern intellectual movement, not merely of an individual opinion); that was the time when a beginning was made with what now appears as the anthroposophical way of looking at things. From this it may be seen that we had in view the extension of the modern tendency of thought to a genuine observation of spiritual reality. We did *not* seek to draw upon the views expressed in publications called at that time (as they are still today) 'theosophical', but we endeavoured to carry forward the aspirations which had originated with modern philosophers, aspirations which had, however, become stuck in abstractions and thus did not gain entrance to the true spiritual world. At the same time, this line of development seemed to me to be an extension of the view which Goethe did not actually express but *felt* to be lying at the foundation of his view of nature, which he described as being 'in accordance with the spirit'. Anyone who has followed my writings and lectures may gather all this from them; and I would not specially mention this matter were it not repeatedly said in error that I have departed from all that I wrote and said formerly and turned to the views represented in the works of Blavatsky and Besant. Whoever carefully studies, for example, my *Theosophy*, will find that everything contained in it is developed in accordance with and as a continuation of the direction of modern thought described above; he will find that the matters dealt with are presented in accordance with certain presuppositions contained in Goethe's conception of the world, and that only in certain places is it mentioned that ideas which I had arrived at (etheric body, sentient body, etc.) are also to be found in literature which is called theosophical. I know that by these explanations I shall not be able to do away with certain attacks that are constantly made against me, for in many cases these attacks are not made in order to arrive at the actual facts of the matter but for some entirely different reason. But what can be done in the face of ever-recurring inaccuracies? Nothing can be done but to reiterate the truth!

*

The researcher who works on the basis of the kind of knowledge indicated in this essay sees that the method of his investigations is in complete accord with the endeavours of present-day natural science. But he knows that these endeavours of natural science must everywhere come to a standstill or run into blind alleys if

they are unable to *meet* what spiritual science can bring to light
from an opposite starting-point. A true view of the matter would
look upon both directions of work as being like the boring of a
tunnel, which commences from opposite directions, but, when
the work is properly arranged, the two parties meet. The *facts* of
contemporary work fully confirm this view. It is only misled
opinions regarding these facts which deny this and presume that
spiritual science and natural science contradict each other. This
contradiction, however, does not really exist. We have a brilliant
example of the importance of the meeting of natural science and
spiritual science in a book which has just been published, in my
opinion an epoch-making book: *Vom Schaltwerk der Gedanken:
Neue Einsichten und Betrachtungen über die Seele* (How thoughts
are controlled. New insights and considerations regarding the
soul) by Karl Ludwig Schleich,[9] S. Fisher Verlag, Berlin 1916. If
you read the important chapter on 'Hysteria — a metaphysical
problem', you will see how a medical research scientist, who is
at the same time a penetrating thinker, confronts facts which can
only be fully elucidated by spiritual science, facts which compel
him to say: 'In the production of tissue through the impulse of
hysteria we have the metaphysical problem of incarnation,' in
'mediumistic vision a kind of clairvoyance which arises out of
disease.' But a person would be under one of the very worst of
illusions if he seriously thought that without the results of
spiritual science he could explain all the actual experiences of
man by the facts discovered by natural science. The scientist who
refuses to consider spiritual science is like someone who has a
piece of magnetic iron in his hand, but has no notion of magnetism and only uses the iron for an implement in which magnetism
plays no part. What would have come out of it if he had put the
magnetism and not the material iron to some use? If you also read
in Schleich's book the chapter on 'The myth of metabolism in the
brain', you will see for yourself how, by sheer force of thought,
the medical research scientist comes to a formal description of
what spiritual science — from a comprehensive presentation of
spirit-life — describes as the etheric body of man. It is interesting
to notice how this particular chapter in Schleich's book shows
that at the present time natural science and spiritual science
often talk at cross-purposes, because the co-operation of natural
scientist and spiritual scientist in intellectual affairs is so difficult

on account of the fragmentation of our intellectual life. Here we come to the painful thought: How different these things would be if scientists were really to become acquainted with spiritual science, instead of passing it by and leaving it to the foolish mis-representations of those who act in accordance with the axiom: Do not examine, but keep your irrelevant, prejudiced verdict! At the close of the above-mentioned chapter Schleich says — and the case is important, because there is no question of ill-will: it is the statement of an upright, true investigator — 'If Goethe, that seer and prophet, observed so many connections in nature and demonstrated that the skull with all its parts is nothing but an expanded cervical vertebra, because all the constituent parts of the latter can be traced in the bony covering of the brain, it would not surprise me if the thought I have just expressed, namely, of the heaping up of the brain out of the elements of the spinal marrow, did not also slip into the labyrinth of his thought. I should not be surprised if some day a slip of paper by Goethe on this subject were found.' Such is our intellectual co-operation at the present time! In 1916 an honest researcher expects that some time a scrap of paper of Goethe's will be found. But this was found by me as long ago as 1891. In the *Goethean Annual* for 1892, p. 175, in the article *Goethe as Anatomist*, written by Professor K. v. Bardeleben,[10] you will read: 'The fact that Goethe occupied himself not only with osteology, but also with the ligaments, the muscles, as well as the brain, is shown by various notes, most of them on loose leaves. In the *Venetian Diary* for 1790 R. Steiner found the following sentence, which may be closely connected with Goethe's thought on the vertebral nature of the skull-bones: "The brain itself is only a large principal ganglion. The organi-zation of the brain is repeated in each ganglion, so that each ganglion is to be looked upon as a small subordinate brain." '. On the basis of this and similar things which I found, I was able to write in 1897 in my book, *Goethe's Conception of the World*,[11] out of purely scientific thought: 'Each nerve-centre in the ganglia was to him (Goethe) a brain at a lower stage of development.' And this, in addition to many other things in connection with it, I have often mentioned since. This is only intended to be a small example of the way in which people talk at cross-purposes in the field of modern science. I shall certainly be the last to reproach Schleich for not knowing the *Goethean Annual* for 1892 and my book of 1897; the uncertainty in our pursuit of science comes not from people but from the conditions.

*

In the present essay it has been pointed out that *all* antagonism to spiritual science proceeding from religious points of view is unfounded. We mentioned the excellent rectorial address given in 1894 by a Catholic priest who was professor to the theological faculty at Vienna University. We are referring to Doctor Laurenz Müllner and his discourse on *Galileo's Importance to Philosophy*. In this address Doctor Müllner, who remained a faithful son of his church, says the following: 'Thus a new conception of the world appeared' — he is referring to the Galileo-Copernican view — 'which in many respects was apparently at variance with opinions regarding which it was asserted, with very questionable justification, that they proceeded from the doctrines of Christianity. It was much more a question of the contrast of the widened world-consciousness of the *modern* age to the more limited one of *antiquity*, a contrast to the Greek, but not to the rightly understood Christian, conception of the world, which could only see fresh marvels of divine power and wisdom in the newly discovered starry worlds, enabling the miracle of divine love accomplished on Earth to acquire still greater importance. ' With respect to the relation of spiritual science to religion it may similarly be said that spiritual science is often apparently at variance with opinions which are represented as belonging to Christianity, but which with very questionable justification assert their origin in the doctrines of Christianity. It is more a question of the contrast of the world-consciousness *of our modern age*, which has extended *into spiritual reality*, to the narrowly limited natural-scientific consciousness of the last few centuries, but not the rightly understood Christian conception of the world, which should only see in the spirit-worlds of Anthroposophy new marvels of divine power and wisdom, where the miracles of divine love accomplished in the world of sense can only acquire enhanced significance. As soon as there is in certain quarters a fundamental insight into spiritual science such as was possessed by the noble priest and theologian Laurenz Müllner into modern natural science, all the attacks which are often made in such an unjustifiable manner upon spiritual science from the standpoint of religion will cease.

HUMAN LIFE FROM THE
PERSPECTIVE OF SPIRITUAL SCIENCE

PREFACE

The following observations formed the content of a lecture given by me on 16 October 1916 in Liestal, which could be thought of as a continuation of the one I delivered in the same place on 'The Mission of Spiritual Science and of its Building at Dornach'. My endeavour in these two lectures was to present as briefly as I could an impression of the ways in which the knowledge collectively known as Anthroposophy or spiritual science can be attained. It was also my intention to give a short summary of certain aspects of this knowledge which pertain to the spiritual nature of the human soul and other related matters.

As with the other lecture, I introduced into what follows some thoughts about objections which have been made from many quarters against anthroposophical spiritual science. These objections often arise in a most peculiar way. For these critics do not take a proper look at what spiritual science says and inveigh against *that*, but concoct a distorted image of what they *think* it says and launch their assault against this caricature. In this way, one often finds oneself attacked, not for what one is actually trying to do but for the opposite, which has never been my aim. Such antagonism is frequently devoid of any serious intention of really getting to know what is being condemned. There is little that can be done with these attacks except to try continually to find new ways of speaking about the true paths and purposes of anthroposophical spiritual science, and from various points of view. This is what this lecture set out to achieve.

Rudolf Steiner
Dornach, November 1916

38

HUMAN LIFE FROM THE
PERSPECTIVE OF SPIRITUAL SCIENCE

Lecture given at Liestal, Basle, 16th October 1916

As was the case with the lecture that I gave here in January of this year, I am far from wanting to make some sort of propaganda on behalf of Anthroposophy through what I shall say today. My intention is, rather, to answer some questions which inevitably arise in this part of the world, where the building in Dornach which serves spiritual science is so close at hand.

A perfectly understandable question for someone who, as an outsider, looks upon the Anthroposophical Movement would be: Is there a reason in the cultural life of the present for the arising of such a movement? One might well understand if such outsiders were to arrive initially at a negative opinion. They may believe that certain people who do not have enough to do come together to concern themselves with things that are useless for real life and have no significance for those who have to spend their time doing practical work in the service of humanity. Such an opinion can, however, only arise if there is insufficient real familiarity with the circumstances of human progress in the course of the last three or four centuries, especially during the nineteenth century and on into our own age. If we cast our eyes over all the changes which have come about in human life during this time when compared with the needs of earlier ages, we become aware of how many new things have been discovered about the working of natural forces. These discoveries have thoroughly changed the whole of human existence and the conditions of life. How different human life is from what it was in the not so very distant past! If we survey our life as it develops from childhood until old age, a different prospect from before opens out. Such a survey shows how we enter into life, how we have to carry out our work and are prepared for this during our childhood and youth. It shows that we then develop the need to know something about the meaning and the real significance of life. We cannot remain satisfied with what we perceive through our senses or with what we do with our hands. In the course of our life we become aware of the voices of our soul-life, and we ask: What significance does this soul-dimension have in the outer, physical world? An initial answer would be, of course: The world gives an ample answer to questions such as these. It adds the element of religion to the content of our outer work and life's experience. Through this element is revealed the eternal significance of what lives in our outer physical nature; it transforms the gate which apparently shuts off our physical life into a gate through which the soul can ascend to an eternal life of immortality.

Generally speaking this answer would be perfectly correct, and it would seem justified to say: Why should it be necessary for something of the nature of spiritual science or Anthroposophy to thrust its way between outer life in the physical world and religious revelation, with its message about man's eternal being?

Anyone who seeks to be lulled by this generally correct opinion into acquiescence with human life as it is now would, however, be failing to take into consideration that the last few centuries, especially the most recent times, have given this life a particular form, which makes it necessary for people at the present time to view all life's questions in a manner which transcends this general opinion. Even in earliest youth, the range of experiences encountered today is quite different from those of earlier centuries. Just consider the extent to which the impressions and ideas that we receive today as we pass through our education and schooling differ from those of former times, for the reason that they rest upon the great advances that have been made in recent centuries and in the immediate present. It lies in the nature of the historical progress of mankind that the circumstances of life change quite fundamentally over certain periods and that only when this change has attained a certain dimension do people succeed in making changes in their soul-life. Thus only in our own time are the soul-questions stimulated by the changes of the last three or four centuries coming to the fore and becoming clearly apparent. This can be seen above all from the faith which many individuals in the nineteenth century were still able to cherish but which our age regards as erroneous.

Not so long ago it was still possible to believe that natural science — which is by no means unappreciated by spiritual science but is as regards its great advances fully valued and admired — had the means to solve all the great riddles of human existence. But those who have entered with heightened inner faculties into the achievements of modern science have been increasingly aware that what natural science brings as a response to the great questions of human existence are not answers but, on the contrary, ever new questions. Human life is enriched by these new questions; but on the level of natural science they remain no more than that. The people of the nineteenth century, academics included, have been insufficiently aware of this. They thought they were receiving answers to certain of life's riddles, whereas these questions were really having to be asked in a new way. These are now our questions. They are present in the souls of people today in so far as they are really involved in life, and they demand answers.

Those who are gathered together in the Anthroposophical Society are generally well aware of these riddles of life, which are not arbitrarily dreamed up but necessarily arise out of what is experienced. These questions are, it is true, particularly apparent in the scientific domain, though they are not exclusive to those who apply themselves in this realm but are the concern of all who enter fully into life as it is today. If answers to these questions were not to be found, certain consequences for human life would result which would bode ill for the future of mankind. A person who speaks in this way at present may be regarded as an idle dreamer. However, such a view will only be expressed by those who are so dazzled by the great advances in human progress that they fail to see that these must be followed by advances on another plane if what is already present within humanity as a potential is not gradually and imperceptibly to become a reality.

It might well be thought that people's perception of these riddles of life is becoming dulled and that these questions are not being posed. But then those mental powers which human beings possess and which aspire to be developed in this way become paralysed. The human soul would then enter into a condition which can be compared with a situation where one's hands and arms are bound and one cannot do anything with them. Powers that reside within us but which we cannot make use of have a paralysing effect on us. And this growing sense of inner paralysis brings about an indifference towards — even a complete lack of interest in — everything to do with soul and with religion. But this situation is not one that can last. Indifference towards the soul is a condition that can only be borne for as long as one's interest is still lovingly sustained by whatever it is which is plunging the soul into darkness. On its own, this interest fades away after a while. It may persist with those who are under the direct influence of the remarkable fruits of modern science; but in the end it vanishes. And as a further consequence, those who are no longer directly under this influence find that they also begin to lose interest in outward affairs. Joy in both life and work falls under a shadow. Life is experienced as a burden.

The first symptoms of indifference towards religious life are clearly to be observed in the nineteenth century. Instead of exemplifying this through one of the many scholars who believed that the questions of spiritual life can be answered by natural science, I shall speak here about a simple man of the people who believed something of the same kind. I am referring to a peasant who during the nineteenth century lived through a kind of martyrdom in Upper Austria: Konrad Deubler[12]. Deubler was totally taken up with the legacy of nineteenth century natural science. In his youth he had for a time been absorbed in spiritual studies of the kind that had emanated from Zschokke[13]. But he was diverted from this through becoming acquainted with Darwinism, with the writings of Haeckel, Büchner and others. He wholly gave himself up to the materialistic views of Darwinism, became completely absorbed in the ideas of Haeckel, and finally came to acknowledge that all talk about spiritual worlds coming from any source other than that of natural science is sheer folly. He believed the world to be formed purely out of material substances and forces. One can have nothing but admiration for the *personality* of Deubler; he became a martyr of his own convictions, for he had to spend a lot of time in prison for them in the fifties, when such a thing was still possible. Deubler was not a person who adopted views out of a superficial impulse but one who was utterly carried away by the tendency of his century to deny all spiritual sources of knowledge. To be sure, he had a zest for life until his death. But this was because he lived in an age when it was still possible to be dazzled by purely scientific achievements. The psychological consequences of ideas such as his only became apparent in those who came after him. Deubler is a notable example of a particular soul-constitution of recent times. Many similar examples could be cited. They would furnish proof of the fact that many people at this time found it possible to believe that natural science offers a comprehensive explanation of world phenomena. It is neither possible nor desirable to forestall the scientific investigation of nature, for this is necessary if modern man is to introduce anything advantageous into his daily life. But if the human mind is directed one-sidedly towards natural science, man loses his connection with spiritual life and with the soul-aspect of his being. Individuals such as Deubler did not as yet realize that natural science furnishes new questions rather than new answers for the life of soul. Their views would have had to become ever more general if a spiritual science that could be the equal of natural science had not been added to it.

Hence those who have come together in the Anthroposophical Society are of the opinion that in spiritual science or Anthroposophy a bond is to be created between the great advances associated with natural science and the religious life of man. If we enter into the real significance of natural science we can say that it leads to a picture of the world in which the essence of man's nature has no place. In saying this I am not expressing my own view, but what becomes clearly evident when we study scientific research with an unprejudiced mind; for only an age which — though with justice admiring scientific knowledge — has been unable to recognize its limitations could deceive itself about this. Individual scientists have long recognized certain limitations; and the speech that Du Bois-Reymond gave in Leipzig in the seventies, which ended with the admission 'ignorabimus', 'we shall never know', has become famous. This eminent scientist meant by this that however much we may investigate the mysteries of nature with the methods of natural science, we shall never ultimately be able to discover what lives in the human soul as consciousness or understand what lies at the foundation of matter. Natural science is of little use when it comes to understanding matter and consciousness, which are in a certain sense the two poles of human life. It could be said that natural science has forced man as a spiritual being out of the picture of the world that it is building up. This can be seen if we take a look at the ideas which have emerged from a scientific foundation regarding the evolution of the Earth.

I know very well that these ideas have been subject to many variations up to the present time and that many people may regard what I am referring to as out of date. That, however, is not the point. What is said along these lines today is conceived out of the same spirit as the old Kant-Laplace theory of which I am going to speak now. According to this conception, the Earth — together with the entire solar system — has been formed out of a kind of primeval nebula in which nothing existed save the forces that such a formation contains. Through the rotating of this primeval nebula the planetary system containing the Earth was gradually formed, and through the further evolution of the same forces which were initially present in this nebula everything that we now admire on Earth (including man) came into being. This view is considered to be extraordinarily illuminating, and it is even taught to children at school. The illusion that it is illuminating is readily accessible, since only a simple experiment is necessary to present the idea to children — and one may then think it has been made clearly obvious. Such clear evidence is loved by all those who try to find in natural science a satisfying philosophy. It is only necessary to take a drop of a substance that floats on water, pass a piece of cardboard through the drop in the plane of the equator with a pin stuck into it perpendicular to this equatorial plane. The drop is allowed to float on the surface of the water and is rotated with the pin. And behold — little drops break away, a miniature cosmos arises! This is said to represent the whole process of the arising of the world in miniature, and children think they understand, for it seems so plausible. But there is always one thing that is left out of account. Although it is sometimes very good to forget oneself in daily life, it is not good to do this in scientific experiments. The drop would not separate off any little drops from itself if the teacher were not there to turn the pin. But since everything that is necessary for the arising of a phenomenon must be taken into account, anyone who demonstrates this experiment must also make it plain that there must have been a giant professor or teacher out there in the universe who stuck a gigantic pin through the nebulous mass and caused the whole to rotate. And anyway, what has arisen out of the drop? Nothing other than what was already there before its fragmentation. Clear demonstrations can therefore be thoroughly deceptive.

It is, however, the case that people with a really healthy feeling for the world have rejected such evidence in spite of all its scientific authority. I shall cite as an example someone of whom I have also spoken in my latest book, *The Riddle of Man*[14].

Herman Grimm, the great literary historian, was of the opinion that Goethe had never in his life had anything to do with the purely external explanation of world evolution. Herman Grimm says: 'Already in Goethe's youth, the great Kant-Laplace fantasy of the origin and eventual destruction of the earthly globe had taken root. Out of a spiralling cosmic nebula — as children know from school — the central bubble of gas which becomes the Earth is formed and, as a solidifying sphere, passes in unfathomable periods of time through all its phases, including the episode of habitation by the human race, in order finally to plunge back into the Sun as a burnt-out clinker: a long but very easily comprehensible process which if it is to come about requires no external interference other than the endeavour of some outside force to maintain the Sun at the same temperature. It is impossible to conceive of a more barren outlook for the future than this prognosis which is thrust upon us as a scientific necessity. A decaying bone around which a hungry dog circles would be a refreshing and appetizing morsel in comparison with this ultimate excrement of creation in which guise our Earth is eventually to home in on the Sun; and the intense craving with which our generation imbibes and thinks it believes such theories is a symptom of diseased imagination, which is to be explained as a phenomenon of the times and upon which learned people of future ages will exercise much ingenuity. Goethe never entertained views of such utter desolateness...'[15].

What Herman Grimm felt — at a time when Anthroposophy could not as yet come to expression — deserves close consideration. For it shows that people have a sense for a different solution to the great questions of existence than the one which natural science — wonderful as it is — is believed to be able to give (though I must again emphasize that spiritual science has no hostility towards natural science). Indeed, the true path of modern science lies precisely in this, that it is in the position to raise far-reaching questions to which, however, answers must come from another direction. It is the aim of spiritual science or Anthroposophy to give these answers. Quite different cognitive powers must be unfolded from those that are recognized today. I spoke about the development of these supersensible powers of cognition in my previous lecture here. I have no wish to repeat what was said in that lecture but wish simply to point out that in addition to the ordinary soul-forces that man possesses and which he makes use of when he engages in scientific research there are others which can also be developed, and that these other cognitive powers are related to the ordinary faculties as, for instance, the musical ear is related to a perception that is directed merely towards the vibrating strings of an instrument. From the outward point of view a perception of a symphony that disregards the hearing of it reveals only vibrating strings and so forth; whereas something quite different is manifested to the musical ear through the vibrations. The spiritual investigator is, in a certain sense, a person who has developed a perceptive faculty with regard to the world which is related to natural-scientific perception as is the musical ear to a perception which is directed solely towards the vibratory processes of space. He develops faculties by means of which the spiritual world is revealed, just as the symphony is revealed through vibratory processes.

I should like to make it very clear that it is by no means necessary for someone who seeks to bring Anthroposophy to fruition in his soul to become a spiritual investigator. The relation of the spiritual investigator to another person who is not himself engaging in spiritual research but only assimilates its results, is not the same as the relation of the scientist to one who studies the results of scientific research. The relationship is quite different, as I shall try to convey by means of this image.

The spiritual investigator himself merely prepares the instrument through which knowledge of the spiritual world is imparted. By unfolding certain faculties the spiritual investigator is enabled to forge instruments by means of which everyone who is sufficiently unprejudiced to use them in the right way may gain insight into the spiritual world. It is only a case of having the right ideas about the nature of these instruments. Whereas a person who prepares the instruments for a chemical or clinical experiment assembles external objects through which a secret of nature can be made apparent, the spiritual investigator prepares a purely soul-spiritual instrument. This instrument consists of certain ideas and relationships between ideas which, when rightly applied, open up the way into the spiritual world.

Spiritual-scientific literature is therefore different in its conception from other literature. The literature of natural science communicates certain results with which people acquaint selves. The literature of spiritual science is not of this kind. It can become an instrument in the soul of every individual. Anyone who permeates his being with the ideas that it propounds is not merely confronted with a dead result which can be learnt, but has something which, through an inner life, unites him to the spiritual world he is seeking. Whoever reads a spiritual-scientific book will — if he reads it properly — observe that what lives in the book can become in his life of soul the means of bringing this soul-life itself into harmony with spiritual existence; and he now comprehends spiritually what he formerly only understood with the senses and with the intellect that is bound up with them. If this is still but little recognized and spiritual-scientific literature is thought to be like any other, the reason lies solely in the fact that we are right at the beginning of the development of spiritual science. As this proceeds it will become increasingly apparent that in a book that is truly written out of Anthroposophy we do not have what we find in other books, but something of the nature of an instrument which does not merely communicate facts of knowledge and through which we are able to arrive at such facts out of our own activity. We must be clear, however, that the spiritual-scientific instrument is of a purely soul-spiritual nature, that it consists of certain quite definite living ideas which, because they are not pictures but living realities, are distinguished from all other ideas. It must be emphasized that even at the present level of spiritual science everyone who aspires to it can to a certain extent become a spiritual investigator. However, this is not necessary if one seeks to make spiritual-scientific know-ledge fruitful for the soul in the sense described.

Just because spiritual science or Anthroposophy is still at the beginning of its development, it is quite understandable, even natural, that the results to which one is led through the devel-oped faculties of the spiritual investigator are met with doubt, smiles and even derision. But this doubt and derision will increasingly disappear in course of time, when the needs that are as yet still slumbering in the majority of people become conscious. Universal recognition will come for spiritual science as it has come for much that has happened to mankind in the course of its evolution.

The spiritual investigator recognizes at the outset that man as he appears to the senses, and to the reasoning powers associated with them, and as he can be studied by a natural science employing outward means, represents only a part of the whole of human nature; and that within the totality of his nature there is a *supersensible* aspect, which lives and works in the physical human being and without which this physical aspect would immediately become a corpse. For the spiritual investigator discovers that just as colour is perceived with the physical eye, so can the *etheric* body be perceived by — to use Goethe's expression — the 'spiritual eye'. The term used, 'etheric body', does not especially matter and I would ask you not to make words a stumbling-block; I could have easily used another one. Within the human physical body the etheric body lies supersensibly hidden, a body which cannot be seen by means of physical eyes but must be beheld with the spiritual eye. It might be thought absurd that the spiritual investigator adds this etheric aspect to the physical aspect. But just as man, as a physical being, has within him the forces and substances — together with their influences — that are in his physical earthly surroundings, so does he also have within him spiritual forces, which he has in common with a spiritual environment. Let us first consider the forces of the so-called etheric body. This consists of certain forces which may be called supersensible. Just as the physical forces which man bears within him can be found by natural science in the earthly environment, so can these supersensible forces be sought in man's environment. But this spiritual aspect of our environment must be beheld with the 'spiritual eye'.

I shall now speak of something which shows the particular relationship that exists between spiritual processes in man's cosmic environment and the forces within man which form his etheric body. As we trace the course of the year with our ordinary faculties of perception, we see the plants shooting forth in the spring and becoming ever greener, and later on developing coloured flowers and forming fruits. We then experience the plants' fading and withering. In nature we perceive alternatively summer's blossoming and winter's repose. This is what is presented to an outward observation of the yearly cycle. But what is thus presented is only related to the spiritual as are the vibrating strings to the musical tones that ring forth from them. The 'spiritual eye' adds a kind of spiritual hearing and spiritual beholding to this alternation of blossoming and repose — which for the spiritual investigator is what the vibrating string is for the musical ear. And as with the physical eye we see plants springing forth from the earth, so the spiritual investigator sees how from the Earth's environment beings move towards the Earth in the same measure in which plants spring from the soil. However incredible this may sound for the modern way of looking at things, it is nevertheless true that the 'spiritual eye' sees a rich life streaming to the Earth every spring from the earthly surround-ings, something which does not happen in winter. Whereas with our physical eyes we behold only the physical plants growing out of the soil, we see spiritual beings, etheric beings, growing down from the cosmic environment. As physical plants grow towards maturity, we see that the living spiritual essence which sinks down into the plant-life of the Earth disappears from the Earth's etheric surroundings. Only when the fruit begins to develop and the flowers fade with the approach of autumn does all that had been united with the Earth, and had in a sense disappeared into the plant-world, withdraw again into the realm surrounding the Earth. And so we spiritually perceive the in- and out-streaming of a supersensible element in the being of the Earth from spring until autumn. It is as though living, supersensible plants were growing out of the etheric world and disappearing into the physical plants.

In winter a different spiritual experience presents itself. A person who experiences winter simply by watching the snow and feeling the cold does not know that the Earth in winter is an altogether different place than it is in summer. The Earth has a much more intense, more active spiritual life of its own in winter than it has in summer. And if we really live into these conditions, we experience the alternation of etheric life in winter and summer; we become aware of a spiritual element which can, in a sense, be compared with what we experience in the alternation between going to sleep and waking up. In this brief description it is impossible to show that these experiences are not at variance with facts relating to the Earth's movements. Anyone who examines spiritual science more closely will soon realize that objections which draw attention, for example, to the fact that the Earth is rotating are of no significance.

Thus we learn that, in winter, certain beings are separated from the Earth and live in its cosmic surroundings, and that these beings descend in spring to the Earth, unite themselves with plant-life and enjoy a kind of repose through being thus united with earthly life. This repose which these beings find within the Earth has, through the fact that a spiritual element has united itself with the Earth, a stimulating effect upon earthly life; and in winter the Earth has a kind of memory of this summer communion with beings of the extra-terrestrial cosmos. Something that we would otherwise be unaware of is revealed to spiritual-scientific perception from surrounding nature; it is as though we were suddenly to develop the power of hearing and were to hear musical sounds ring out from the vibrating strings which, because of deafness, we were previously unable to hear. We come to know etheric life. This etheric life shows that certain beings of the Earth's surroundings who are connected with other cosmic bodies unite with the Earth during the summer and withdraw again during the winter. This life requires that the Earth — if we regard it as a being and not as a dead body, which is how it is viewed by geology or by natural science in general — sleeps during the summer but is awake during the winter, with living memories of what has been united with it in the summer. The conclusions about earthly life that we may reach through analogies of one kind or another are the direct opposite of the truth. Such conclusions would lead us to believe that the Earth wakes up in spring and goes to sleep in autumn; whereas spiritual science brings the insight that the warm sultriness of summer represents the Earth's time of sleep, and the cold period when the Earth is covered with snow represents its time of wakefulness. Anyone who understands such an experience in the right way will no longer see fit to object that the comparison with musical hearing proves spiritual science to be merely subjective, like artistic interpretations in general. For the consequence that is introduced into the earthly organism of what has been beheld over the summer is an indication of the objectivity of the process.

Let me emphasize that spiritual science, unlike certain philosophies of the nineteenth century — that of Fechner, for example — does not build up anthropomorphic ideas but gives the results of what it beholds, which are real spiritual perceptions; and these are for the most part very different from anthropomorphic conceptions. This would enable certain antagonists of spiritual science to understand how little foundation

there is for confusing it with a philosophy of an anthropomorphic stamp. If we permeate ourselves with the knowledge that
stems from these observations, we learn to understand how
human life itself is fashioned; for of all the riddles that confront
us in the outer world, human life itself is the greatest.

In a short lecture I can only give a brief indication of what
Anthroposophy has to say about the riddles of human life. I
would, however, like to speak of a rhythm which it discerns
therein. The first section of this rhythm is the period of childhood
— the period from conception to birth, interesting as it is, cannot
be considered here. This is the time from birth until the remarkably
interesting phase of the appearance of the second teeth, that is,
until approximately the sixth or seventh year.

So much develops in this first period of life that educationalists
of discernment have said:[16] An individual learns more from his
mother or nurse in his first years of life than he can learn from all
the peoples of the world during the rest of his life, even if he were
to travel all over the globe. During these years the human being
acquires, among other things, the capacity to stand upright, the
faculties of speech, thinking and memory; and there also takes
place the nurturing of those inner powers which find fulfilment
with the appearance of the second teeth. All these processes of
development appear before the spiritual investigator as called
forth by earthly forces. He must, of course, add all that the
'spiritual eye' beholds within earthly evolution to what the
senses are able to perceive in the realm of Earth-existence. But
what takes place within the human being until approximately the
seventh year can be understood out of the sphere of the forces
that are to be found in the earthly realm. This does not, of course,
imply that spiritual science has already investigated all the
mysteries of this period of human evolution, but simply that if an
investigation is to be really thorough it will have to seek what is
being considered here within Earth-existence.

A second phase of human life begins with the change of teeth,
and lasts until roughly the fourteenth year, that is, until the
onset of puberty. As regards this period, spiritual investigation
finds that the processes which unfold within the physical body
are no longer to be explained from what is operative on the
Earth itself, but from extra-terrestrial forces that are of a similar
nature to those that have been described in connection with

plant-life in the course of the year. This extra-terrestrial, or etheric, life exerts an influence in the second period of human life in such a way that the process which for the plant-world of the Earth is enacted in one year takes about seven years in man. This is not said out of some kind of mystical interpretation of the number seven, but out of the results of spiritual observation. It must be emphasized that the forces that are at work in the second period of human life are only *in a way* similar to those which influence the growth of plants from the extra-terrestrial realm. In the case of the plant the extra-terrestrial forces do indeed exert an influence from without but, whereas the same forces are active within man, this influence is not actually exerted in a spatial sense. What works etherically in the unfolding and decay of the plant-world in the course of the year lives as though enclosed in the human organism as the etheric body. The developmental process of the second period of life from the seventh until the fourteenth year takes place under the influence of these forces. Through the fact that man has within himself the forces for these processes of development, he is no longer a mere earthly being but the image of an extra-terrestrial sphere, albeit only as it exists in the realm of the senses.

In the case of the brain, we have an organ that is pre-eminently the product of earthly forces. It seems so strange in the light of the usual modern conception of the brain to think of it as essentially a product of earthly forces. Outwardly, this is manifested through the fact that at around the seventh year the human brain has reached a kind of conclusion in its development — not, of course, in the development which consists in the assimilating of concepts and ideas, but in its inner formation and structure, the hardening of its parts and so on. Something must now be added to what has until the seventh year played a part in the development of the human body, something which is not contained within the earthly realm but has its origin in the extra-terrestrial sphere, and which brings it about that from the seventh to the fourteenth year the forces which man develops in regions of his organism other than his head and brain also rise up to influence the development of his head and countenance. With his seventh year, the individual as it were gives birth to a super-earthly, etheric aspect of his being, which works within him in a free and living way. Just as his physical body enters into physical existence with birth, so now an etheric, super-earthly body comes into being. The result of this is that what is expressed in the facial features is brought to greater clarity. Through the etheric body the breathing and circulatory systems also take on a more individual character. And as it is no longer only earthly forces which are active in the physical organization but also the etheric body and the formative influences of the extra-terrestrial aspect of man's nature, that inner quality unfolds which thenceforth accompanies the human individual throughout his subsequent life as the bodily expression of his mind and feeling-life.

There is, however, more to human nature than this etheric body which man has in common with the plants. When spiritual research is directed towards the animal world it finds there another supersensible element, which — unlike the supersensible aspect of the plant world — is not to be found in the extra-terrestrial environment. This is a spiritual reality which can be found neither in the earthly nor in the extra-terrestrial realms. It is a supersensible element which is already present in man from birth, indeed from conception, but it only begins to exert an influence on the bodily organization from approximately the fourteenth year. It is not active, as are the etheric elements, in the region surrounding us as earthly human beings.

As I have already said, spiritual science enables us to become aware that in winter the Earth retains a memory of what it has experienced during the summer in connection with extra-terrestrial forces. As we learn more about the spiritual nature of the Earth, we shall discover that the Earth-body on which we now live is a descendant of a pre-earthly planet, as a son who has descended from his father; but whereas a son resembles his father in form, the Earth-body is the descendant of another planetary being with which it has but little resemblance. We come to know this planetary being if we can contemplate the Earth in winter when it, so to speak, wakes up and develops a sort of memory. For in the spiritual element which is revealed within the Earth, a memory-picture is still preserved of the stage passed through by that cosmic body which afterwards became the Earth.

These things sound paradoxical today — to many people, foolish or even mad; but so it has been with all those matters which have subsequently been recognized in science as perfectly obvious. In the cosmic body that was the Earth's predecessor there was no mineral kingdom. It is a considerable step for spiritual science to have taken to come to the recognition of the fact that the Earth has evolved out of a planetary predecessor where the mineral kingdom did not exist. The etheric element which exerts an influence today from beyond the Earth and which is united with the Earth only during the summer was not so separate from the Earth's planetary ancestor as it is from the Earth as it is now. This ancestor from the time before the mineral kingdom developed was a being which was itself alive. It was in its entirety a living being.

If the 'spiritual eye' is able to see how the present Earth has arisen from an earlier living predecessor, it also becomes able to discern that supersensible element which works as such in man and in animals, and which can be found at present neither in the earthly nor in the extra-terrestrial realms. It is operative in animals and, in a higher way, within man. The human organism is the bearer of this supersensible element from birth, and it has been fashioned in such a way that it can be its bearer. From about the fourteenth year this supersensible element begins to manifest a distinctively *independent* activity which was not present before; and as a result of studying this activity with the 'spiritual eye' it becomes possible to distinguish a third member of human nature, the astral body or soul-body — again it should be borne in mind that the name is of no particular consequence and could be replaced by another. It will at first be difficult for someone who is not really familiar with such trains of thought to form an idea of the difference between the astral body before and after the fourteenth year. This and other difficulties can only be overcome through becoming further acquainted with spiritual science.

In approximately the twenty-first year another supersensible member begins to exert an influence upon the human organism. This is the real bearer of the *ego*, of the human self, a member which raises man above the animal kingdom.

With regard to this member of man's being it must be asked in what sense Anthroposophy maintains that it only begins to manifest an independent activity in the fourth period of life, since it is apparent that man owes to it the attributes of upright posture, speech and so on which raise him above the animal kingdom already in childhood. The solution to this apparent contradiction emerges from a knowledge of the particular supersensible nature of the human ego. Man is so organized that, on the one hand, the *independent* manifestation of the ego in the bodily organization only takes place in the fourth phase of life, whereas on the other hand the ego evolves through repeated earthly lives. If the ego only possessed the forces which can be acquired in *one* earthly life, the unfolding of these forces would have to be delayed until the body makes this possible in the fourth phase of life. But it enters into earthly life having already had previous experiences; and the forces which equip it for repeated earthly lives enable it to work upon certain parts of the bodily organization in such a way as to manifest itself in the manner referred to before the fourth phase of life. For this same reason, the astral body can, through the ego, also be active in the physical organism earlier than would otherwise be the case.

Just because spiritual research is able to perceive the difference in the way that the ego works within the human organism before and after the onset of the fourth phase of life, it recognizes that man's existence on Earth passes through repeated lives, which are separated by long periods of purely spiritual existence between death and a new birth.

I have given an outline of one aspect of the anthroposophical view of the world. As it would take me many hours to convey an adequate impression of the path of research lying behind the thoughts that I have here expressed, this cannot be more than a mere sketch. You may perhaps realize from what has been said that this is not based upon the arbitrary use of fanciful speculation or philosophizing, but upon careful and conscientious research requiring specially developed faculties of perception. Through this research, what natural science is able to say about man's bodily nature is supplemented by a knowledge of the spiritual element which surrounds us every bit as much as our physical environment surrounds us as physical beings.

In this world which opens up to us through spiritual research we first encounter beings who grow down etherically to the Earth just as plants physically grow forth from it. We have in these ether-plants the first precursors of spiritual beings and spiritual powers with which we become associated, just as through our senses we become associated with the physical world. But as we come to know the spiritual world, that world whence the human astral body and ego have their origin, we become familiar with a spiritual world with real spiritual beings who surround us, a world to which we belong in our souls just as in our bodies we belong to the physical world, a world where dwell those who have passed before us through the gate of death. It should be emphasized — I have already spoken of this in the previous lecture — that there is no question of spiritual science seeking a relationship with the dead that arises out of mere capriciousness. If we are to approach a dead person, the initiative must come from the dead person himself. It may then be possible that through *his* will we receive from him a revelation of the 'spiritual eye', just as we receive other knowledge from the spiritual world. Everything which proceeds from this realm must be approached by the spiritual investigator with a reverent reserve. But such knowledge as may flow to us from the spiritual world through the conscious unfolding of our faculties is *our own* concern, and contains answers eagerly sought for by those who — in the sense of the present lecture — feel the spiritual needs which arise naturally in the present epoch of human evolution.

Just as this epoch of evolution has led to a new knowledge of nature, it is equally necessary that it leads to spiritual science. Increasing numbers of people will recognize what is today still widely disputed, that spiritual science does *not in the least degree* detract from religious sensibility, from the religious life of man, but on the contrary seeks to form a bond that will again unite scientific man with the mysteries that are accessible to him through religious revelation. True spiritual science is not in any sense opposed to natural science, nor can it estrange anyone from religious life.

Natural science has recently become aware that it is itself a great question, that something needs to be added to it if it is to be truly comprehensible. If I now speak of the fact that natural science is out of its depth when it ponders the riddle of man, I am not basing this on my own view of natural science. Personal views such as this have no real place in spiritual science, which does not encourage one to speak out of subjective considerations but allows the way things develop to speak for itself. Thus I should like at this point to speak of what the recent historical development of natural science has itself brought to expression. I refer to a fact that sheds considerable light upon scientific developments in recent times.

The great hopes placed on Darwinism, spectral analysis and the advances in chemistry and biology were developed to a particular degree in the middle of the nineteenth century. At the end of the 1860s, Eduard von Hartmann wrote his *Philosophy of the Unconscious*[17]. The author of this book was not as yet a spiritual investigator but was — through hypotheses, sometimes thoroughly illogical hypotheses — pointing towards something which will only really be revealed by spiritual science, towards a spiritual essence behind the physical world to which he gave the controversial name of the 'unconscious'. He intuited philosophically certain facts that can be established through spiritual science. Because he philosophically presupposed the spiritual, he was unable, in spite of the imposing stature that materialistic Darwinism and natural science as a whole had acquired in the sixties, to agree with what scientists of the time generally believed, that a knowledge of physico-chemical forces and outwardly perceptible biological forces renders any view about *spiritual* forces of activity unscientific. He therefore tried to show that what is acknowledged by Darwinism points towards the ubiquity of spiritual forces in the development of living beings.

And how did certain scientists respond to what Eduard von Hartmann propounded? Generally, as certain people today have received what spiritual science propounds, especially those who have become so accustomed to a natural-scientific view of the world that they regard everything that does not harmonize with their own views as confused nonsense. People such as this who believed, when Eduard von Hartmann came on the scene, that they alone possessed the truth, declared: Well now, Eduard von Hartmann is a mere dabbler; he knows nothing about the nerve-centre of scientific research, so no one should allow himself to be led astray by this amateurish *Philosophy of the Unconscious*. Many responses appeared, all of which referred to Hartmann as a dabbler; they wanted to show that he had no understanding of what natural science has to say.

Amongst the many responses there was one from a man who at first remained anonymous;[18] it was a thoughtful contribution, written out of the truly scientific spirit which Hartmann was challenging. This criticism of his scientific follies seemed to deal

Hartmann a devastating blow. Eminent scientists said something along these lines: It's a shame that this writer has not revealed his identity, for he has the spirit of a true scientist, he knows what science is about. If only he would give his name, we would regard him as one of us. This judgement of the scientists contributed much towards this pamphlet being rapidly sold out. After a short time a second edition was necessary, and the hitherto anonymous author was named; and the author was none other than Eduard von Hartmann! That was a lesson to all those who seek to condemn views alien to their own after the fashion of the scientific opponents of Hartmann. Thus Eduard von Hartmann showed that he could speak just as scientifically as the scientists themselves. And the spiritual investigator of today could, without much effort, speak in a similar way about all that has been said by those who condemn him as an idle dreamer, as someone who is far removed from scientific thinking. I mention this not in order to indicate how one or another person is to be responded to, but rather to show how things often stand with the refutations that are openly directed by people who pride themselves on their scientific rectitude against insights other than their own.

There is, however, more to be said on this subject. One of the most eminent pupils of Haeckel — thus of that figure who stood most radically for the materialistic views of Darwinism — Oscar Hertwig,[19] who has written a whole series of books on biology, presents in his latest and highly significant work *The Development of the Organism: A Refutation of the Darwinian Theory of Chance* a picture of the total scientific impotence of a materialistic Darwinism in the face of life's essential questions. In this book a proof is given from the standpoint of a scientist that the hopes that Haeckel and others have placed upon Darwinism's capacity to solve the great questions of life were unfounded. (I want to make it quite clear that I still value what Haeckel has done for the philosophy of modern science just as much as I did years ago. I believe, as I have always believed, that a true appraisal of Haeckel's achievements leads far beyond his own one-sided views — though it is understandable that he himself does not see it this way.) Oscar Hertwig often quotes Eduard von Hartmann in his book; and he cites opinions of Hartmann's which decisively refute what has been said by the erstwhile Darwinist opponents of this philosopher.

Incidents such as these show us how the philosophy of science
has developed. Its most eminent exponents today clearly indicate
how it has gone completely astray in recent years. This will
become ever more widely known; and with the recognition of
this fact will also come an understanding which will not only
point towards what Eduard von Hartmann and the speculative
philosophers had to say about natural science, but will also be
able to recognize what spiritual science has to add to these
scientific achievements. Infinitely much could be brought forward in this way to support the view that the true scientific mode
of thinking is at present in complete harmony with spiritual
science. And it can truly be said that there is no more contradiction
between Anthroposophy and the religious life than there is
between Anthroposophy and natural science.

I said something of importance in this respect in the first
lecture that I gave here. It is my conviction that no one who
earnestly considers the views expressed in that former lecture
will have any misgivings about Anthroposophy from a religious
point of view. I should like today to make one point in order to
show that those who stand within the thought-life of a particular
religious confession cannot raise any objections to spiritual
science if they are people of good will. I shall show how spiritual
science may be considered from the standpoint of the philosophy of Thomas Aquinas,[20] who is fully recognized by the Catholic
Church as a Christian philosopher; and what I have to say in this
respect could also be applied to the relation of a Protestant way
of thinking to Anthroposophy.

The philosophy of Thomas Aquinas distinguishes between
two kinds of knowledge: firstly, there is the knowledge that flows
unconditionally from divine revelation, knowledge which man
accepts because he sees in this revelation the reason for its truth.
Truths of this kind are — according to Thomas Aquinas — that of
the Trinity, the doctrine of the chronological beginning of earthly
existence, the doctrine of the Fall and of the redemption by the
Incarnation of Christ in Jesus of Nazareth, and the doctrine
concerning the Sacraments. According to Thomas Aquinas, a
person who understands the nature of his cognitive powers
should not try to fathom these truths by means of cognitive
activity that he unfolds from within.

In addition to these matters of faith there are for Thomas

Aquinas also those truths which man can attain through his own cognitive powers. These truths are the *praeambula fidei*. Amongst these he numbers all those truths which relate to the presence of a divine-spiritual power in the world. Thus the existence of a divine-spiritual Being who is the creator, ruler, preserver and judge of the world is not merely a matter of faith, but an aspect of knowledge that can be attained by means of human faculties. Also belonging to the realm of the *praeambula fidei* is everything that pertains to the spiritual nature of human existence and, in addition, all that leads to a distinguishing between good and evil, together with the knowledge which furnishes the foundation for ethics, natural science, aesthetics and anthropology.

We can be wholly in agreement with the view of Thomas Aquinas and recognize on the one hand that what is a matter of faith is not in any way altered by Anthroposophy and, on the other hand, that everything which Anthroposophy propounds falls within the realm of the *praeambula fidei*, if this conception is understood in the true sense of Thomist philosophy. In the view of Anthroposophy, there are areas of knowledge lying quite close to man which must be treated in the same way as are the matters of faith on a higher plane. In ordinary life we have to receive certain things as a result of information which we are unable to experience for ourselves, for example, the knowledge of what has happened to us between the time of our birth and the point of time to which our memory goes back. If, as a spiritual investigator, a person develops spiritual powers of cognition, his vision extends beyond this latter point of time; but before that period of development to which the memory normally goes back the 'spiritual eye' does not see events in sense-perceptible form but instead beholds all that was happening in the spiritual domain while the corresponding events were taking place in the physical world. Sense-perceptible processes *as such*, if they are not made conscious through experience, can only become part of spiritual knowledge if they are communicated to it. No healthy-minded spiritual investigator will, for instance, believe that he should dispense with what is communicated to him by his fellow-men and seek to reach the same insights by spiritual observation.

Thus, as far as Anthroposophy is concerned, there are, even in the realm of ordinary life, aspects of knowledge which are dependent on information. On a higher level, the 'matters of faith' recognized by Thomas Aquinas are related to processes which are inaccessible to a human knowledge resting on its own powers alone, because they live in a domain beyond ordinary experience which, like the processes occurring in physical existence in the years immediately after birth, does not fall directly within the compass of spiritual vision. Just as knowledge of physical processes is only received through information from other human beings, so can the processes and events that correspond to the 'matters of faith' only be known through information (revelation) from the spiritual world. The fact that spiritual science employs such concepts as the Trinity and the Incarnation in the sphere of spiritual perception has nothing to do with the application of these notions to the region to which Thomas refers. Moreover, anyone who understands Augustine will realize that such a mode of thought cannot be called unchristian.

Thomas Aquinas' view regarding the *praeambula fidei* is also reconcilable with Anthroposophy. For everything that is accessible to self-sufficient human powers of cognition must be recognized as *praeambula fidei* . Thomas includes in this, for example, the spiritual nature of the human soul. If, through an extension of knowledge, spiritual science augments the insights concerning the soul that are disclosed to the intellect alone, it is simply extending the scope of that knowledge which falls within the domain of the *praeambula fidei* ; it does not step beyond this realm. In this way it attains to truths which give firmer support to 'matters of faith' than those obtained merely by the intellect. Now Thomas' view is that the *praeambula fidei* can never penetrate to the sphere of 'matters of faith', but that they can uphold (support) them. Therefore, what Thomas requires of the *praeambula fidei* is fulfilled all the more by their extension through spiritual science than through the intellect alone.

My purpose in making these observations about Thomism was merely to show that it is possible to be a very strict adherent of this philosophical persuasion and yet be fully in agreement with spiritual science. Naturally, I do not mean to suggest that everyone who accepts what spiritual science has to give must embrace Thomism. Anthroposophy does not interfere with anyone's belief; and whether a person belongs to this or that confession has nothing to do with what he knows about the spiritual world, or thinks he knows, but with other circumstances of his life. The more these things are understood the more will hostility towards Anthroposophy disappear.

Those who have worked their way to a recognition of Anthroposophy today will find comfort in the opposition that they face when they realize how it has been for certain other ventures which, because of the utilitarian principle, have had an easier path in the world. In the nineteenth century railways were introduced into the cultural environment of the time. An administrative body — such as had the authority for these matters — had to pass a judgement in a certain place as to whether a railway was to be built or not. The story has often been told[21]. Apparently, the decision was that the railway should not be built since the health of those who travelled on it would suffer. And if the would-be travellers wanted to expose themselves to this danger and railways were to be built for them, high board fences would have to be erected on both sides of the line so that the health of those whom it passed was not endangered. I mention these things not out of mockery towards those who were one-sided enough to pass such judgements. It is, after all, possible to be a person of great importance and yet make a mistake of this kind. If one finds that someone is opposed to what has been undertaken, one should not without further ado label this opponent foolish or malicious. My motive in speaking about the opposition that so many have experienced is, rather, that if those who are exposed to it can see it for what it is they will be able to adopt the right attitude to it.

It would be difficult today to find anyone who would not be delighted to hear Beethoven's Seventh Symphony. When this work of art was first performed, Weber, no mere nonentity but the celebrated composer of *Der Freischütz*, made this remark: 'Now the extravagances of this genius have reached the *non plus ultra* — Beethoven is ready for the mad-house!'[22]. And when Abbot Stadler heard the same symphony, he expressed himself thus: 'He keeps on repeating the E, and the stupid fellow doesn't even notice!'[23].

It is certainly true that even those who have not achieved notoriety in this way are very glad to refer to such incidents. Not of course that they *prove* anything in any particular case. But the purpose in mentioning them here is not to prove something but rather that they may stimulate a closer examination of much that seems strange before judgement is made.

Such things can also be set in a greater context. In doing this, I am of course very far from wishing to compare the work of Anthroposophy with the greatest of all events in human evolution. If we consider the development of the Roman Empire at the beginning of our Christian era and the growth of Christianity from that time onwards, we see how remote Christianity was from everything that was then considered worthy of the interest of educated people in Rome. From this Roman culture we then turn to look at what was going on literally under the earth in the catacombs. And then we look at what took place a few centuries later. Christianity has risen up from the depths, it has been accepted in those regions where it was formerly despised and rejected. Considering such events can bring confidence to those who believe that they should serve truth, even where it has to struggle against opposition.

A person whose being is permeated with Anthroposophy will not be surprised when there is opposition; but he will regard it as his duty to respond ever and again by placing what Anthroposophy potentially represents for the cultural life of humanity in its true light.

SUPPLEMENTARY NOTE

The brief references to objections made by opponents of Anthroposophy which I have included in this lecture are in the nature of general discussions and do not deal with specific instances. If one were to go into detail, one would indeed have some strange things to say. For example, a pamphlet appeared recently[24] containing the report of a lecture that was given in Switzerland; and the following can be read in it about the relationship of what I said in this lecture to Christianity: 'Thus again we return to the challenge made by the Russian mystic Solovyov, that we can and should all be Christs — a challenge that has been made by all mystics who have seen fit to take heed of Christianity.' This was said in 1916 about my spiritual-scientific teachings, in spite of the fact that anyone who has dipped into my book, *Christianity as Mystical Fact*,[25] or has paid even superficial attention to what I have said subsequently on the subject, will become clearly aware that this is an objective falsehood.

Another example. Although it should be clear from all my writings that I am striving towards a mode of research which aims at the complete extermination of all suggestion and anaesthesia, the following can be found in the same pamphlet from which the sentence quoted above is taken: 'We can only be grateful to Dr. Steiner for showing us the extent to which suggestion and anaesthesia play a part in modern mysticism.' By this is not meant that I am showing how suggestion and anaesthesia can be overcome, but that I have succumbed to them. So it is with many 'refutations', which of course only go to show that people first make a suitable caricature out of what they are attacking and then launch their assault against this caricature.

NOTES

1. Robert Zimmerman, 1824-1898; aesthete and philosopher. From 1861 until 1895 Professor of Philosophy at Vienna University. One of the leading representatives of the Herbart School. cf. *Anthroposophie im Umriss. Entwurf eines Systems idealer Weltansicht auf realistischer Grundlage* (An Outline of Anthroposophy. A sketch of a system of idealism on a realistic foundation.) Vienna 1882. See also Rudolf Steiner, *The Course of My Life*, Anthroposophic Press, New York 1970, Chapter 3.

2. *Mysticism at the Dawn of the Modern Age*, Anthroposophical Publishing Co. 1928. Also published as *Eleven European Mystics*, Rudolf Steiner Publications, New York 1971.

3. Helena Petrovna Blavatsky, 1831-1891; founded, together with Col. H. S. Olcott, the Theosophical Society on 17 November 1875 in New York, though its centre was soon afterwards transferred to India.
Principal works: *Isis Unveiled* (1877); *The Secret Doctrine* (1887-97).

4. Annie Besant, 1847-1933; after the death of the first president, H. S. Olcott, in 1907, became President of the Theosophical Society.
Works: *Ancient Wisdom* (1898); *Man and his Bodies* (1906); *Esoteric Christianity* (1922).

5. 'In the dramatic presentations...': The original performances of Rudolf Steiner's four Mystery Plays took place under his direction in Munich before audiences composed exclusively of members of the Theosophical, subsequently, Anthroposophical Society:

The Portal of Initiation	15 August 1910
The Soul's Probation	17 August 1911
The Guardian of the Threshold	24 August 1912
The Souls' Awakening	22 August 1913

The performance of a fifth mystery play was planned for the summer of 1914. As in previous years, Rudolf Steiner intended to write it down before the beginning of rehearsals. Then in August the First World War broke out. The festival had to be cancelled and the play — which he had fully worked out in his mind — was never actually written.

See *Four Mystery Plays*, Rudolf Steiner Press, London 1982.

6. 'how Giordano Bruno had to appear before humanity': cf. *De l'Infinito, Universo e Mondi*, (1584), fourth dialogue: 'Thus there exist infinitely many worlds, not in the way that one imagines the Earth to be surrounded by so and so many spheres, some of which support one, and others countless stars, but rather do all these great starry worlds revolve in a free, open space...'

7. 'Although it is highly gratifying...': Ignaz P. V. Troxler, *Vorlesungen über Philosophie*, Bern 1835.

8. 'In a lecture...': Held in Berlin on 8 October 1902 (not translated).

9. Carl Ludwig Schleich, 1859-1922: doctor and writer, friend of Strindberg.

10. Karl von Bardeleben, 1849-1918: anatomist, professor in Jena.

11. *Goethe's Conception of the World*, Anthroposophic Press, New York 1928.

12. Konrad Deubler, 1814-1884; cf. *Konrad Deubler, Tagebücher, Biographie und Briefwechsel des oberösterreichischen Bauernphilosophen*, Leipzig 1886.

13. Heinrich Zschokke, 1771-1848; writer, statesman and educationalist.

14. *The Riddle of Man*. Mercury Press, Spring Valley 1990.

15. 'Already in Goethe's youth...': Herman Grimm, *Goethe*, Stuttgart and Berlin 1903.

16. 'Educationalists of discernment have said': Jean Paul (1863-1825) in *Levana oder Erziehungslehre*, Stuttgart and Tübingen 1945. The relevant passage runs as follows: 'Every new teacher has less effect than the previous one, until finally, if one were to regard one's whole life as an educational institute, a globe-trotter would receive less educational benefit from all nations put together than he does from his nurse.'

17. Eduard von Hartmann: *Philosophie des Unbewussten, Versuch einer Weltanschauung*, Berlin 1869.

18. 'Amongst the many responses...': *Das Unbewusste vom Standpunkt der Physiologie und Descendanztheorie. Eine kritische Beleuchtung des naturphilosophischen Teiles der Philosophie des Unbewussten*, Berlin 1872.

19.   Oscar Hertwig, 1849-1922, anatomist, pupil of Ernst Haeckel; the work in question appeared in 1916 in Jena.

20.   Thomas Aquinas, 1225-1274, Dominican, scholastic, church father in Cologne. Pupil and friend of Albertus Magnus. Between 1262 and 1264 he led the papal theological seminary in Rome and from 1265 until 1267 also the studies of the Dominicans. From 1268 onwards he taught in Naples and Paris.
Principal work: *Summa theologica*.
See also Rudolf Steiner, *The Redemption of Thinking*, Anthroposophic Press, New York 1983.

21.   'The story has often been told': See also Rudolf Steiner, *Practical Training in Thought*, Anthroposophic Press, New York 1974.

22.   'Now the extravagances': see August Göllerich, *Beethoven* (1904).

23.   'He keeps on repeating the E': ibid.

24.   A pamphlet appeared recently: W. Joss, *Moderne Mystik und freies Christentum*, (published separately by the Swiss Theological Journal (Zürich) XXXIII, year 1916, vols. 2/3 and 4.)

25.   *Christianity as Mystical Fact*, Rudolf Steiner Press, London 1972.